Denice

Thank you so much
I truly hope you read
something that touches
your heart.

2018

Book design by Ashley Branch

Photography by Ashley Branch

Intro

To all those known and unknown, welcome. I am more than honored that you have found interest in my poetry. However, you will find more than just poetry here. You will find gems that has shaped me into the artist that I have become. You will enter into a realm that will unleash my theories and beliefs. Such as my concept that poetry has purposely written me. This voyage will be more than ocean deep as it takes you from my humble beginnings to my most current of writings. This voyage will be one that does not diminish but challenges your own theories, concepts, beliefs, ideologies, etc. Only for the sake of expanding your mind and heart through the work of art. All are welcomed upon this journey as you are accepted in your totality. For writing has forced me to push my pride aside so that you may have a transparent view of me. My strengths, my weaknesses, my secrets. Truth is I am tired of keeping them. I have written a book full of tears yet no one knows how much I've cried. A box full of suicide letters and no one knows I have contemplated my life. A blueprint to success yet no one knows the mountains I've climbed. All of this must be revealed in hopes that it helps another to survive. This is a book written from the heart of an empath. There is no need for judgmental human ears. Know that whether Good, Bad, or Ugly to your Truth these pages have listened.

Love

Love

Love. A four letter word that is intriguingly complicated. A word most misunderstood, questioned, and misused. A high of sorts that once reached and lost you will spend the rest of your life trying to find it. A challenge that I have faced in many chapters of my life yet haven't quite mastered. However everyday I continue to learn. What I have come to learn for sure is that you are nothing without love. Love is essential from the day of conception until your last breath escapes you.

Love for me is best compared to planting a tree. It starts with a seed and when you plant that seed you look for fertile or rich soil. Once planted, you water and foster it along daily with the care of mother nature. The seed will then sprout. You will continue to raise and water that sprout all while cultivating the ground that it is embedded in. The result, a healthy tree. The tree will then have grown bearing produce, providing shade, filtering out toxins, providing oxygen and even shelter. It will weather many storms. The branches will be strong and even if one breaks it will not be a sore to the eye, but it will actually add to its beauty. On the other hand if you take that same seed. Plant it in bad soil. Deprive it of your care, rely solely on mother nature, and if you only cultivate the ground that it is embedded in sparingly. Your tree will grow just as malnourished as you treated it. There will be little to no produce. The produce may lack quality. The tree may not produce enough branches and leaves to provide shade or filter out toxins. It may not be able to withstand storms. It may fall effortlessly and broken branches will be easily noticed. As it will be an eyesore and confirmation of disparity.

This same concept applies in every relationship you build and honestly in everything you do. For what is the worth in having or doing if you do not love what you have or do? The answer is nothing. Value increases due to appreciation or in other words the love you have for it. Therefore any and everything you can conceptualize must be conceived with love, cultivated with love and surrounded by love. In doing so the very foundation of it will be strong and solid just like the roots of a tree. Your any and everything will blossom and the produce you will reap will be beneficial and plentiful. The toxins will filter themselves out so that you may be able to enjoy the shade and breathe easy. Anything that may harm or hinder what you have built will not be a sore to the eye but will add to its beauty. Storms will envy the triumph that it has withstood over them. Anything other than this will become just as malnourished as it was treated. For nothing is worth digesting if love is not the main ingredient whether it is mentally, physically, emotionally, etc.

This comparison has so many sectors to it that if I were to elaborate on each one it would become its own book. For instance we can go into how the seemingly bad tree can be saved given the right amount of patience, compassion, and work ethic. We can reflect on who you are as a tree. Just like people each tree is different and requires its own type of care and surroundings in order for it to survive. I have used this comparison to analyze myself and my relationships. Using a tree graph to dissect how I or any of my relationships have grown from the roots on up. It will honestly help you reveal a lot about yourself and your relationships. As it creates a perspective that is more sound than silent.

There is a saying that "the heart wants what it wants". Even so, knowing that the heart is foolish I believe that the heart needs what it needs. I am in no way, shape or form an expert on love. I still search for advice myself. Though when all else has failed me the best advice I have ever received about love and what it is, was from Gods' word the Bible. Specifically scripture 1st Corinthians 13:4-8 "Love is long-suffering and kind. Love is not jealous, it does not brag, does not get puffed up, does not behave indecently, does not look for its own interests, does not become provoked. It does not keep account of the injury. It does not rejoice over unrighteousness, but rejoices with the truth. It bears all things, believes all things, hopes all things, endures all things. Love never fails." Even when you do, love doesn't! How beautiful is that? It is so unconditional.

Love as warm as a child's heart is necessary in such a cold world. I know it isn't easy due to all the pain that exists. But the demand is high just for that reason. So please just try to love! Love daily! Understanding that every circumstance and situation is different you can still love accordingly. Love from afar, love by letting go, love by holding on, but at the end of the day just love. For love truly conquers all.

Love

Love
What is it?
It's magnificent
Infinite
I know its more than a stroke to the clitoris
But intimate
Celibate
And relevant to this lifetime,
This family, this relationship, this future
Our God ...
Is Love

When Love gave Love to Me

When love gave love to me
It was a sight to see
For love had never abandoned me
Or commanded me to be nothing more
Than me
And love appreciated everything
That I beheld
Even if I wasn't feeling well
Love could tell
And love would just love me harder
And even when I tried to test love
Love became smarter and loved me stronger
And then I stopped trying to test love
And adored love
Because love was true
See when love gave love to me
It was unconditional
And love wasn't afraid or scared to give
Because love gave until his heart bled
And said that all I had to do was receive
Because when love gave love to me

There was no compensation fee
For love gave love to me for free
By putting a roof over my head
With a pot to piss in
And when I'm hungry
Love supplies me the whole kitchen
See love, loved me so much
That he would die for me
To make sure that I had enough soul for resurrection
Love was my armor and my protection
Forget joy
See I am elated
Because all love did was give me simple pleasure
That hit me so deep
It made things complicated
Love overrated
No see it hasn't even began to reach its peek
For there is no limit to the love
That love seeks
And love loves me
To the point that it caters to my addiction
Allowing me to get higher
See love has become my number one supplier
For love has become the essence of my
Desire to speak
So when one gives love to me
It's only the completed act of loves destiny
See when love gave love to me
It gave me the power to keep love
Loving eternally

Boyfriend

Boyfriend you one hard working pimp
got every girl blowing up like a blimp
then you only thirteen and ain't got no job
got your baby mamas praying to the lord above
Boyfriend you ain't only saying sorry to Mrs. Jackson
you saying sorry to the whole clique
Mrs. Lawrence, Mrs. Foster and the lady down the street
with the patent leather whip
See boy, you done messed up a whole lot of people's lives
the sisters don't know the brothers
the brothers don't know the sisters
what if they become husband and wife
then you got baby mamas becoming grandma too soon
she didn't expect her babies stomach to blow up like a balloon

Consider Me

Consider me as your friend
consider me as the one who will stick with you till the end
consider me as one who cares
consider me as a person who will always be there
consider me as someone who is humble
consider me as a person who will sometimes stumble
consider me as a person and nothing else
because that's who I will always be and just myself
so consider me

Missing You

When you are not here,
it seems like everything is unclear
Why? Because I'm missing you
When I'm all alone and no one's home
I want to call you on the phone
Why? Because I'm missing you
You know in the dark
I start to miss the way you talk,
the scent of your clothes,
and the way your eyes spark
Though in all my days
I would never say how missing you would
make me crave
Then when I see you again my world begins to spin
and I ask myself if missing someone like this is a sin
Though it comes as no surprise
that missing someone this much will lead to better future ties
Why? Because I'm missing you

I Knew

I knew your favorite color
and you knew mines too
I knew you would believe me
whenever I told the truth
I knew you would help me
whenever I fell down
I knew you would uplift me
and get me off the ground
I knew you be there
whenever I needed a friend
sometimes I even knew that
you would be there till the end
but what I never knew
and had to learn to know
was how my best friend
could become my worst foe

My Type Of Man

He's that cool, type of calm, kind of sweet
type of man
that will do anything for his peeps
type of man
he's that person you would really long to meet
type of man
he's my type of man
he's that run his comb and fingers through his hair
type of man
kind of laid back with a glassy stare
type of man
so strong but emotionally tender, yes he's a rare
type of man
he's my type of man
see he's that brownish and reddish original skinned
type of man
native decent, black soul, special grin
type of man
he's more than a father or a friend
type of man
he's my type of man
he's that after him I want to name my son
type of man
if I call no hesitation he will come
type of man
before him no numbers come because he's that #1
type of man
he's my type of man
he's that creative minded and very wise
type of man
that will hold me close and wipe my tears if I cried
type of man
he's the one I want with me when I rise
type of man
he's my type of man
he's that father figure with an old soul

type of man
who will let you know whatever he knows
type of man
he's that I want to watch you reach your goals
type of man
he's my type of man
he's that strong carpenter, kind of fix it
type of man
that will sing while he works or just whistle
type of man
if he ever left me I would miss him
type of man
he's my type of man
he's that looking up at the stars, smoking and drinking beer
type of man
that will listen to whatever I have to say because he doesn't just hear
type of man
he's the one I would nominate for person of the year
type of man
he's my type of man
he's that Smokey Robinson and Temptation listening
type of man
I Love Lucy watching, big pimping, slick talking
type of man
strolling while he's bopping, almost George Jefferson walking
type of man
he's my type of man
see this man, a real man
a made that was made for me
yes he's my type of man
and I will forever call him Granddaddy
Dedicated to my Grandfather

Dealings

I dealt you the King of life
the Queen of souls
and I dealt you the deuce
I gave you the Jack of riches
the Ace of beauty
and I gave you the King of freedom
So you could let loose
I dealt you the 10 of Love
the 9 of strength
and the 8 for head starts
But what you gave me was a great surprise
for I received the Joker of Hearts

Unexpected

What do you expect of me?
Want me to give you all the attention
do something for you
just because you mentioned it
be there every time you call
give you everything or nothing at all
be everything you ever had
your mom, sister, brother, and dad
want me to be there to wipe your every tear
want me to be your confidence and face your fear
want me to play your game
say your name, be the one who never complains
be your voice to speak
your eyes to see
your nose to smell, your hands to touch
want me to hold you tight and love you so much
want me to be your slave, and fill your cup with ice
be your all and never think twice
want me to be your mind to make your every decision
your hopes, your dreams, and all your wishes

it's hard to understand what you want me to be
I know I'm your friend but really what do you expect of me?

Confusion

So many people confused
now I'm skeptical of the friends I choose
and all the people I love their trust I lose
and for what reason
they change more bluntly than the seasons
when did I deserve to be treated with treason
I'm tired of the truths untold
and sin being so bold
and something so new to me
quickly becomes old
but I cannot give up I have to hold up my head
grab on to their hand and
keep them from going off the edge
but they've just stop standing and have fallen instead
but I feel their confusion
because I'm confused with them
it's so many people changing
I wonder if I'm committing the sin

Willing

I know your games, but I don't complain
because my heart and soul you are filling
and like a fool I am willing
I'm willing for you to play me like the game I am
and make me commit to sin
for you to hurt me like you've done the others
because your spell I am under
I know about how you did the dirt you did
but I swept it right under the rug like a little kid
you give such a good vibe in all the wrong places
so I go along with it, but reality I can't face it
the adventure and sin of it is wrong
but so thrilling
I guess that's what makes me so willing

Pleasurable Deceit

This is the taste of Eves fruit from Paradise
Sending one to hell
this is having the trust and faith of one
to keep a secret
but that's the one who opens his mouth to tell
it's looking into the beautiful
eyes that kill
and the wait for a promise to happen that never will
it's the lure of a kiss that sets ones heart on fire
but the heart that burns is far from desire
it's the want of something so bad
that it sets one up to fail
it's the hug that feels so good but
no one can feel the hands piercing the back
with its deceitful nails
it's the feeling so right about
something so wrong
and having something so good to you
that really doesn't belong
it's the feeling that feels so good it makes you
close your eyes and takes you into another land
it makes one feel so weak that their knees buckle
and they can't stand
it's the walking up to heaven
and meeting Satan at the gates
and it's receiving something so lovely
that soon becomes something one hates
it's the outcome of negativity
that gives positive energy
that should last forever
but this concept I still sit and ponder
Is how deception gave me pleasure

Cruelty of Money

Money can replace a broken car
but it can't replace a broken heart
Money can replace all material things
from the house that I live in
to a precious wedding ring
Money can replace money itself
but the cruelty of money will only bring you wealth
Money can replace anything that nature can't bring
but it's funny how you let the cruelty of money
replace you and me

In The Eyes Of The Beholder

In the eyes of the beholder
lies my interest in you
lies the lies and lies the truth
in the eyes of the beholder
are all the confessions of each connection
and the response of deep affection
in the eyes of the beholder
is a picture that only ones eyes can see
that will lead one to its destiny
in the eyes of the beholder
is a sign that one is receiving of either a heart that is good
or one that is deceiving
in the eyes of the beholder
it may not appeal to you and me
but in the eyes of the beholder
holds a place of truth and honesty

Temptation

I have a sensation knocking on my door
and it hurts so bad he makes me sore
sometimes he's a foe sometimes a friend
that's why I'm contemplating if I should let him in
he sets my soul on fire
not a burning pain but a burning desire
Sometimes he controls your actions and emotions
takes so long he moves in slow motion
you know he's wrong, but you think he's right
got you thinking so much you can't fall asleep at night
see knocking on my door is a sensation
it's not pain, or love, his name is
Temptation

Scared to Love

I want to love those who say they love me
and the only thing stopping me is the fear of being deceived
I want to know what love is all about
from the caring, sharing, into the passion, but all I have is doubts
I am filled with curiosity
and it's bundled up inside of me
I look for love but why can't I see
the passion that takes me to ecstasy
but what am I looking for a passion or mutual agreement
when I'm fiending for the chance to be intimate
but I can't be another man's victim
I have to stay innocent
oh, how I yearn for the experience to make love work
but I'm scared to love for the fact it will feel too good
and the fear that love will hurt

Don't Leave

We have been through worse
we have stared death in its face
we've laid in the hearse
so, don't leave
don't leave the love and lust
the loyalty and trust
the me, the we, the us,
you can't
see you can't leave the hand that feeds you
the taste that pleased you
you can't leave the One that needs you
And you …
you need me,
We need we
just why can't you see
that the door is not open
so, you can't leave

Can't Get None

Yea our eyes connected and you acted too sweet
It was the first time in a long time
I've been swept off my feet
But by me being blinded
With your words that were mesmerizing
And me realizing
You trying to be more than a friend
Forcing yourself in
To a place where the mark would be permanent
I'll admit the entertainment would be fun
But me and you could never be one
And from a challenge I never run
But politely saying
You can't get none

All He Wanted

He wanted me to trust him
And that I did
He wanted me to hug him
And that I did
He wanted me to kiss him
And that I did
He wanted me to miss him
And that I did
Until it became an end
And he found another friend
While I was trusting him
But when he wanted me to trust him again
I tried
I wanted
I said I did
But that… I didn't

Mommy

Mommy this is for you
For dealing with all the things that a mother
Shouldn't have to
For you I wish I could turn back the hands of time
So, I could erase all the bad things that have hurt you inside
You were always true and you were always there
Even though there were times that I questioned If you cared
But you always came through
That's why I never want to be the one to hurt you
I know I may do wrong things and they may seem foul
And the excuse is not bearing me as your child
I just want you to know sometimes things get wild
And I promise to try my best to make your days worthwhile
There were a whole lot you could've stopped but you let it
And there's a whole lot you have done for others
And for that you received no credit
Just let it be known that through my eyes
You have been recognized
For being a strong woman making it through hard times
Yes, you survived
You have survived from the one I call beast
From the long hours that you stand every day on your feet
For those nights when you couldn't sleep
And for those days you couldn't eat
And your body felt weak
This poem is for you because I want you to know
That you are deeply appreciated
And your presence makes me feel elated
Because I don't know what I would do if the difference
Between life and death kept us separated
Mommy, it just feels so wonderful when you and I
Are us
That's why it hurts so much to know I have lost your trust
But once again mommy this is for you
for doing all
The things a mother shouldn't have to

Class of '05

Yesterday was a mystery
Tomorrow we will make history
But today we are present
So, let's unwrap the gift that City is giving
And enjoy this land of plenty
Because we are receiving much more
Than the average person is getting
See today there are 2005 reasons for the choir to sing
And 2005 reasons for the band to play
And 2005 reasons for us to throw up our ring
Because what we bring is more than 300 strong
And more right than we've brought wrong
Yes this is what we have longed
To finally approve and congratulate
All those we appreciate
Because not the upcoming but following spring
When we show off our cap, gown, diploma,
And once again our ring
And not amount to the average
But to the far more greater things
Yes, this is for what we aim
And the world around us is what we claim
They said '05 is our name
And a symbol of unity
That's why I say explicitly
Tomorrow we will make history
But today we are present
So, let's unwrap the gift, the ring,
That the class of '05 is receiving

Nights

Nights are what we spent together
Though no one knows if these nights will last forever
So, this night I spend with you
I want to do all the things I wouldn't
Normally do

Hidden Emotions

It feels like I'm on an emotional roller coaster
My emotions so twisted got me feeling drunk
When I'm really sober
My eyes look open to all those on the outside
When on the inside, I'm blind
And to you I'm smiling
Remember though a smile is deceiving
Because on the inside I'm frowning
About everything displeasing
And to you I'm breathing
When I'm on my last breath
And to you I seem apart of the living
When I'm really on my last lifeline to death
But you really don't know
Because all the feelings I really feel
Are different than the ones I show

Falling In Love

I try to dodge it
Hoping this feeling wasn't true
And I found myself doing things I wouldn't normally do
Like trusting what I don't want to trust
Or wanting something I don't want
OK I can understand a little
But why so much
Why I want to touch what I don't want to touch
Or think things that I don't want to think
Or feel things I don't want to feel
Why am I having all these emotions inside
That I don't want to reveal
All the things I don't want has happened
And as sorry as I am to say this
it's a mutual reaction
I know how I speak it seems like I'm falling apart
But the place I've fallen is in another person's heart
And I've tried to run
And I've tried to dodge
But I've managed to slip
And I've fallen in Love

Taken

You've taken my cries for joys
And you've taken my joys for cries
You've taken my dreams as doubts
You've taken my truths as lies
You've taken the words I love you
And said it in vain
And even though you have taken so much
It's funny how you decided to give me pain

You

In a very short period of time
You stole my heart
It became a surprise
Because you were the first of your kind
Who put a piece of my puzzle together
And haven't taken it apart
You mean so much to me
That I want to be your shield and your protection
I followed a star and it pointed me in your direction
There were so many from which to choose
But you were my selection
So to you I give my affection
And all my loyalty
And if I could I'd give you all the finer things
But until then I'll give you my thoughts, my soul
I give you all of me
It didn't take that long to see
That you were meant for me
You've seen my joy and you've healed my pain
From your comfort these feelings I've gained
And all I want is for you to feel the same
And even if you don't
Well I still have hope
It's funny because I never felt like this before
My mouth says you're just my friend
But my heart and mind says that
You
Are so much more

Something Special

Words can't describe what we have
It seems like the right words are the wrong words
And the wrong words can't be the right words
I feel like there are no words that are good enough words
To say what needs to be said
But I'm going to take this chance
To say how I feel
I never knew a person that was so real
Who could geek, who could chill,
Who could accept what they deal
Whose heart was so filled with love
Man I pray to the Lord above
That he would never separate the U and S that made US
Forget sisters we are the twins that could never be touched
I give the first words and you finish up
Forget the whole game I know you will be down for me in the clutch
And I never asked for much
But to me much has been given
And what makes it so funny is that our friendship
Is just at its beginning
And it feels like I've known you forever
And together forever we've been living
Sometimes just to talk to you would turn a hell into heaven
Sometimes you changed my whole mind frame
When I be going through things
It's like I could be stuck on one word
And you'll help me finish the page
And the best thing about it is that the roles can change
If I'm listening you're talking and if I'm talking you're listening
As long as I'm here you'll always have food to eat,
A roof over your head,
And a pot to piss in
I would give my life to make sure you had enough soul for resurrection
I say these things because I know you will do the same for me
And these words have no thank you fees
They're all for free

If anything a thank you is coming from me
For making me see how good of a friend you could be
And inspiring me to keep up with my creativity
I swear no matter the struggle
No matter the pressure
We will always have something special
And even though it's the beginning
I cant wait till the end
To show the world that we are still best friends

Word Game

He said tell me what you want
In a man
And I will be all that you'll
Ever need
And I replied
I want to fall in love with a man
For who he is
And not for who he's trying to be

Last Chance

To not understand
The pain inside hurts even more
To not understand
The heartache I must endure
To not understand that it takes more than a day
To fix what has been broken
For you to look into my eyes
Like it's not hurting
To know that you could just
Take away from my pain
Instead of being there through my trials
Not understanding why I want you to stay
To deal with the pressure of right & wrong

And wanting you even still
To give you a choice
And not to understand how time kills
Or what it reveals, or what it would take
For this depth of time to heal
Just think about how I feel
For you to give it up at your own will
Would have been a blessing
But for me to give you a choice
Is so stressing
But you don't understand
Concerned with only your pressures and plans
Though through all that
I'm still giving you a chance
But if I must fall again
By your deceitful hand
I will drop you
Like Hitler dropped thousands In
Concentration camps
Like the twin towers on 911
When the plane hit
Drop you
Like a ball out of bounds
In the last three seconds of a championship
Drop you
Like you dropped my heart
Because you obviously didn't care about it

Forgive and Forget

People have played with my emotions
rubbed the dirt in my face like lotion .
told me every lie
even made me cry
told me they were sorry
and that they never meant it
but in their actions they never repented
gave me reason after reason why they act this way
and told me day after day that they would change
these people say they're my family and friends
whatever happened to the saying
I will be there till the end
now they want to lean on my shoulder
and say I'm sorry over and over
and ask for me to forgive them
for their betrayal and sin
but the pain still hurts and it's already hard enough
I wonder how God can deal with this stuff
it seems like the more you betray me
the harder it gets
so this time I will forgive you
but don't expect me to forget

Interest

I wanna give a shout out to my interest
And I hope I don't offend you
When I spit this
See I know your not perfection
But I'm attracted to your blemish
This attraction that caused a poetic reaction
Got me googling cupids chemist
I need an explanation for these feelings
It's rare that I want an associates friendship
The mystery of the Scorpio
Has caught the Capricorns attention
And I like it
The beauty within your beauty
Is enticing
I can see it with closed eyes
Internally hypnotized
The way you've boggled my mind
And messed up my smooth
It takes me long to respond
Because I've lost the words to appropriately speak to you
The heat is always on no longer cool
Dang! I just don't get it
You're just my interest
And I wanna feel you with no hands
Into my world I want to invite you
If there is a load on your shoulders that is too heavy
I'll remove the weight like lipo
And if our hearts were ever to crash
We don't need to be insured by Geico
Because I promise we will always be progressive
So don't think I'm trying to wife you
Well at least not right now
Just trying to give my interest
A humble shout out
in hopes
That it makes you smile

Title-less

I found myself drowning in shallow waters
Falling immensely in our relations
But the density of our depth
Kept us from sailing ship
See we remained on the surface
But intention kept me paddling
In these puddles intensely
Exhausting myself in waters that
Were barely knee deep
See passion kept me swimming hoping
I could escape the sand
But the lack of connection would never
Keep me afloat that's when I realized
That in shallow waters I could stand

Title-less

We taught each other to live breathless underwater
After our panting heartbeats couldn't swim the
Depth of this ocean anymore
We let go
Broke climaxes barriers
And we touched souls
The high of what life after
Death feels like
A resurrection of connections
Where I was able to be passionate
About passion
An experience beyond compare
Is what we shared
A world I never knew
Yet you met me there

Easy To Love

Never thought I'd be, thought I'd be
Falling for you so easily
Never thought I'd be, thought I'd be
Falling for you so easily
See you are so easy like Sunday morning
Simple like morning stretches
Easing the nights tensions
You are the magnitude of happiness taken for granted
No wonder why I was still wishing
But luckily the past didn't realize it's blessing
Didn't see the precious gift that God had concealed in you
See you are so beautifully packaged
A gift to me that I will take my time unwrapping
Because I want to explore all of you
See I want your sweet nectar
Your morning dew
I want your venom and your ailments too
See I wanna be your armor
Let me take on whatever pierces you
So that it never pierces you again
I take on this challenge
Because you are so easy like balance
The perfect 69 the way we are so level headed
See whatever is on your brain, I get it
When no one else gets it
See that was a doubleheader, get it
See I must admit that even though amazing
It bothers me how I'm falling for you so easily
Because you are so captivating like music
You are my music
You are the perfect picture with sound
You are my muse
So inspiring every time you come around
That I want us alone together on the Daily
Making Marsha Ambrosia's passion so good
That it's Anthony Hamilton amazing

That I need it often more often than the Weekend
I'm talking intimate nights no sleeping
And I won't tell nobody
See I will Ginuwinely tell them ain't none of their friends business
The way I Alicia Keys lock your secrets
Because your secrets are safe with me
I swear I never thought I'd be
Falling for you so easily
But you are so easy to enjoy
Like my favorite artist
I swear every song of his makes me think of you
If you wanted me to break it down
It would be e.g.
That you are my P.Y.T that's so MJ B.A.D
That you became my Thriller
Would give Butterflies every time you pass me by
But I remained a Smooth Criminal
I swear Love never felt so good
But every time I look into your eyes
You make me Remember The Time when we fell in love
See I told you to give me that ring finger
Cuz girl I Wanna Rock With You all night
And A Couple of Foevers Chrissete Michelle
Creating our own Wale Matrimony
Because Baby I got plans for you
Like creating our own Zion
Without any Miseducation
See I wanna build an Empire with you for sure
Because you're so Beautiful
And I don't care who knows
And through our
Up downs, up downs, up downs
I believe that we will always remain in sync
See all this cuffing I was doing and
You were the missing link
To compliment who I am my style
See you got my wrists on clink clink
You can call it lock down and

I swear I never thought I'd be
Falling for you so easily
But who could call it falling when I feel like I'm floating
Gliding on cloud 9
See you are so nurturing, comforting, stress free
It's amazing how I didn't have to pass away
To experience resting in peace
See baby I call you Buddha
Because you bring out the peace in me
You are serenity
And I swear I never thought I'd be
Falling for you so easily
because you are so easy to Love

Title-less

Don't you want some poetry
That's a little more intimate
Like let me tongue
Be soft braille to your clitoris
See I want your body to Stevie Wonder read
The Zane in me
Make you cum literally
Because I aim to please queen
On your cuisine I will dine
Until I got you twitching like a roach
That just got sprayed with pesticides
See I just don't put in work
I put in overtime
I'm talking no days off
Pick up shifts on holidays
Just to get that double time
I'm talking about hard work
Like croutons on lunch time
Call that crunch time
But I ain't tossing no salad
But I will make you cum rapid

Quicker than your dolphin
And your bunny rabbit
Yes I gets it in
Have you going back telling your toy provider
That those tricks were for kids
See you got a player in me for life girl
Don't act like you don't know
Because this point guard
Has won championships and scholarships
The way I split your defense and penetrate your hole
See I keep these niggas mad at me the way
I score with just a finger roll
See I have interesting tricks that inquiring pearls
Would like to know
But they scared to find out about it
Just remember that curiosity
Killed the cat
And I'm the type of cat
That will have that pussy screaming murder
From the closet
Said I only hit it one time
And I killed all nine lives

Victorious

Victorious
all hail loves warriors
for we have never seen
a history of war like this
fighting night after day
no matter how unsure life gets
literally shed blood, sweat and tears
for hearts righteousness
I say all hail loves warriors
for our generation now
wouldn't be able to comprehend
the generation from back then
and their constant battles with forced separation
their desperation of escaping
in strange places
just to see their significant others faces
just imagine their endurance,
their tolerance, their possession of patience
these courageous, beaten, battered
and beyond bruised crazy fools
would become strange fruit
before giving up would be the reason
why they would lose loves battle
overjoyed with just jumping over the broom
made many envious, made others swoon
over what was initiated
the biggest jump that they have ever taken
would be the one that would make a statement
and forever be celebrated
for surviving all their trials and tribulations
no matter how much another race hated
their love has been emancipated
sweet victory
yet constantly we repeat history
free by law
but still enslaved mentally

by this embedded hatred
passed down from generations
and we have let this self hate make us
create our own karma
see then we were fighting for our freedom
now we are fighting the drama
of lost and incarcerated fathers
mothers who just don't want to be bothered
broken homes with tarnished souls
who bear unripe fruit
that bear unripe fruit
you can't win a war of love
when you think the answer is to reproduce
not only does the self battles exist
our lives are still at risk
due to daily attacks of racial genocide
suffocating from economical pesticides
believing in society's stereotypes
that black love cannot survive
and to be honest
we go so hard to keep from seeing weakness
that we become so strong
that we break our own bonds
so now that you understand the enemies
that we are up against
it becomes rare that we prevail
and keep our own race as our preference
but for those who do
for those who accept the challenge
who aren't afraid to suit up for battle
for those who didn't let society
impact their hearts journey
for those who accepted love because love was worthy
for those who didn't let their past hinder their future
I say all hail loves warriors
for black love is the epitome
of beauty that love and war possesses
how beautiful it is to see

them ride an emotional roller coaster together
to mend broken homes
and become mothers and fathers
to kids that aren't theirs
never letting finances weather their storms
when it's cold outside they hold each other to keep warm
and they embrace the rain
for they know who reigns
and the reason they will never reach defeat
because when the loads becomes too
much to carry
they lay their burden at the feet
of their Lord and Savior
Commander and Chief
for when black love survives the war
it becomes Gods prophecy
like the Bible states specifically
1st Corinthians 13:7&8
"It bears all things believes all things, hopes all things
Love never fails..."
Black Love Prevails
VICTORIOUS
ALL HAIL LOVES WARRIORS!

Wedding Piece

Our connection was an automatic
chemistry that linked us together
but we were blinded by the bonds
that were molded
we are a force never to be broken
we were chosen
by our impurities
for the strength in you
saw no glitch in me
a genuine formality
that overrides my flaws and all
you have accepted me
Dear Deverick Sean Murray
I am humbled by your essence
stomach still in knots
at the sight of your presence
in awe in the way you have rescued me
from the darkness of my own suppressions
by your acceptance
the fear of my own demons seem so adolescent
to me you are a testimony of Gods forgiveness
for those days I didn't feel so blessed
through you he has shown me that there is no sin
in just being myself
and I've never felt so free
I love your brown eyes because
they look at me without critique
I love your broad shoulders
because they are there for me when I feel weak
I love your chest for the heart that it holds
loving me more with every beat
see even though I am a
rubrics cube of complexities
you've figured me out completely
with simplicity
you left no color un turned

and let my square into your world
and that is why I love you
I love you for being king enough
to handle the queen in me
my attitude, my strength, my pain,
my love, my accomplishments,
my regrets, my personality
so surreal is my reality
when it comes to you
sometimes I wonder if I'm still dreaming
when I'm up under you
and if I am I hope I never wake up
instead I hope you join me in my inception
and let me love you flaws and all
as if it were perfection
know that I trust you to point me
in any direction and I will follow
understand that my pride I will swallow
just to secure that there is an US tomorrow
see forever and always will be our motto
a promise sealed with a kiss
the people will watch and stare
as we create our own holy grail
this is our Genesis
our beginning
for only God can put together
something so fitting
something so necessary
the life I had before
holds no torch to the one we will carry
because the fire we make is the intensity of love
and the light of clarity
so ladies and gentlemen
friends and family
may you stand for me as I step forward
so that we may take this journey to eternity
as we will stand and make a promise now
that will last to time indefinite

promising to never let any pessimist
be of any relevance
promising as loves warriors we will survive
for the fact that we know our potential
we will forever be fruitful no pesticides
for we are too deeply rooted
to let anyone test our grounds
see no matter how successful we become
we will always remain humbled head bowed
never letting violence be an option
or leaving be the resolution
we are promising to let patience be our answer
and God be our solution
this union is assurance
that there is no conflict between my mind and my heart
for the first time they agree
for the first time
I am not being coupled off
but I am synchronizing my soul becoming one entity
we are becoming whole
and as I stand before you
with swollen eyes because these tears
of joy are out of control
for we are making the promise
to catch each other when we fall
to accept each other flaws and all
and that is why I love you
and that is why I love you
and that is why I DO
Dedicated to Deverick & Kelli Murray

Loves Masterpiece

It isn't easy making masterpieces
creating the perfect picture on blank canvas
it isn't easy putting a bull on a Libras scale
and creating balance
but when fate takes cupids challenge
it relieves this story of all coincidences
for it was purposeful
that the windows of your soul
caught my eyes in a place called common vision
see we had lunch there
and with all that surrounded us
nothing could distract my view of you
see it was then that I beheld your beautiful
it was then that our colors
started dancing across the canvas
with rhythm and blues
see we made music in hues
we painted this canvas
with the colors of lust, tears, insecurities,
trust, love, laughter
we painted this canvas with chapters
of our doubts, the colors of angers flame
the countless mistakes we've made
the uncertainty, the colors we wish we both could erase
instead we kept what we couldn't change
and we kept painting
learning how to love each other better
still creating the perfect picture
that could never fit into a frame
retiring from the game
with back to back to back championships
3 rings
that symbolize how far we've came
our many promises
that at anytime I am your O and Defensive line
having your fullback

leaving no loose strings the way I tight ends
see I am ready to play more than my position
for the position we play in each others lives
now become endless
I am ready for that infinite commitment
of constant roller coaster transitions
creating our own definition of love
something that many can only dream of
creating beauty that isn't intentional
but somehow meant for you- us
showed me that dreams do come true
this love is a dream come true
and my favorite cliche
the way it expresses itself so consistently
why wouldn't I be ready
for our art to forever coexist
having murals of bliss in our midst
yes I am ready
to make masterpieces
creating the perfect picture on a blank canvas
I accept the challenge of putting
a bull on a Libras scale and creating balance
fate has accepted cupids challenge
and I am ready for 2 words 1 consonant
2 vowels 1 vow
at this moment right now
I am ready
I do
Dedicated to Ashley & Tay Branch

The Tree

Have you ever stopped to think about the tree
you know, the tree that bears the fruit
that is good enough to eat to feed the soul
the tree that provides the shade
the tree that even when you don't have a pot to piss in
it lets you soil its fertile ground
yet it still stands strong
naw seriously I really wanna know
have you ever stopped and thought about that tree
I'm talking about the tree that bears the fruit
and how many people its fed without a thank you
have you ever thought how bruised that tree maybe
how many branches have been broken
how many secrets have been kept
by the tree that bears the fruit
that is good enough to eat to feed the soul
by the tree that provides the shade
that tree that even when you don't have a pot to piss in
it lets you soil its fertile ground
yet it still stands strong
but with all that it has been giving
in what way has the tree received
when was the last time this tree had some TLC
I mean like a hug from the core or
when was the last time you watered its fertile ground
how about a simple thank you
or do you even know if this tree is still standing now
see how does one prevail
that has been so neglected
but see with all the neglect in the world
God reigns
God rains midst, showers, storms and even floods
that tree drowning all others in the abundance of its blessings
see I have been that tree
I have been that tree that bears the fruit
that is good enough to eat to feed the soul

I have been that tree that provides the shade
The tree that even when you didn't have a pot to piss in
I let you soil my fertile ground
the tree that in a world so toxic
I provided the oxygen
see I let you breathe easy
I kept your secrets
I withstood the bruises, and broken branches,
the fallen leaves
see I gave all the good in me
without receiving the proper TLC
but with all the human neglect in the world
God never forgotten me
as he rained midst, showers, storms and even
flooding me drowning all others in the abundance
of his blessings
see that is how I was able to keep standing
like the tree who bears the fruit
and all I really wanna say is thank you!

Forgiveness

Why don't you just admit it
that you did, what you did,
when you did it
there's no need in pretending
no use in sparring my feelings
your apologies don't matter if you meant it
and even if you didn't
unfortunately, pain won't allow
me to know the difference
it would be easier to act like none of this ever existed
but even healed wounds leave scars
so that you never forget it
however I just don't get it
father how could you remove yourself
from the puzzle
like I wouldn't realize that a piece of
me was missing
mother how could you preach about love
and not give the same love to all of
your children
and you, you the worst of them
manipulating your image
got me jumping through hoops
just to prove that I am genuine
exhausting all of who I am for you
to only discover
that your true colors
were more fucked up than a Rubik's cube
See I was just another carcass you carved up
to look like a damn fool
but making myself carry the load of these
grudges is cruel
and honestly I just don't have the energy
to continue blaming you
so I decided to fix it
let my real eyes, realize, real lies

so no longer will I buy into a hundred
that's counterfeit
see I stopped blaming chemistry
for the bonds with no substance of character
stopped blaming physics
when it came to my heart
for not filling the space that mattered
and the law of attraction
for not reciprocating the energy I was after
instead I decided to practice forgiveness
to refrain from being sickened
from that hurt people hurt people syndrome
See it's a rather serious condition
where victim becomes villain
and the innocent endures their vengeance
on situations that no longer exist on the surface
but is embedded within their system
too late is usually the time frame
that they realize their afflictions
and the main excuse they conjure up
is "hurting you was never my intentions"
along with "i told you I was broken from
the beginning. I was protecting the pieces
of me that needed fixing"
through your tears became their cleansing
as they begin to find solace
in watching someone else endure what
they have been feeling
even in their repentance
they are consistently inconsistent
with change
one might believe that they are completely insane
because no matter how hard you try to reveal
to them of their monster
they will never see what you see
for their reflection only mirrors mirages
they are completely lost in their pain
have you ever had to suffer from this

sickness
were you the one suffering from being
sick and tired
or were you the one enduring the
sick and tired's vengeance
or were you the one who didn't know
that you were suffering at all
because you were too consumed in your
resentment
I am a testament and a witness
of generations so full of hatred
because of all the scars they have accumulated
that they don't believe in the bruises that they imprint
the new scars to a new millennium that they invent
but see I want pain so far away from me
that I can't feel or see it from a distance
so regardless of mistake or intention
I refuse to continue this saga
I have already taken my losses
so no matter how many tears you made me cry
no matter how many times you left me ghost
no matter how many dreams of mine you've
crushed
I forgive you
to every person who chose to break my heart
to my every oppressor and child molester
to every killer of a friend/ family member
your pain I will always remember
but I forgive you
for not only you but for me
for that well known and simple fact
that I am imperfect
for every time that I have
and unfortunately will inflict pain
upon a person
whether on purpose or unintended
I too pray that I am forgiven
I would hope that they didn't take

my apology as if I never meant it
even though I understand that
pain sometimes doesn't allow you to
know the difference
I would hate for another to lose
themselves due to this sickness
so I am choosing not to be a victim
to all those who have
trespassed against me
no longer will I hold it against them
it is time for new beginnings
therefore you all are forgiven

~You strum on each one
leaving not one nerve unplucked
but no matter how many nerves
you struck
you were a nonsense that was
necessary
you were my nuisance
and together we made beautiful music~

~I am never alone
but often times I am by myself
solitude is nice
but most times I wish I could be close
to someone else
among people is when I feel abandoned
only because I don't want company
I want a companion~

~I want to feel the feeling
that it isn't a feeling
it's real~

~If you love me
what are you waiting for
they say that true love is too strong to ever ignore
but I feel that you love your pride more
because you hold it harder
than the one you say you adore~

~Once I removed my heart from my sleeve
I had less chips on my shoulders~

~Love yourself most when it ain't easy
when you feel you are too hard to Love~

~Love should never hurt
but the hurt that I have endured is
assurance that I have Loved~

~Love for self is the best arrow cupid could've
ever shot me with,
for that is the only reason that I continue to have love for you~

~Got a hand full of hearts but people keep cutting them
you tryna set the game
I just want to book one of them~

~Never treat a nickel like a dime
because they'll start acting like a dollar
forgetting they owe you change~

~Be thirsty enough to swallow your pride~

~Frustrating when you are the one for everyone
but you can never find the one for you~

~Love gets lost in translation
when two hearts don't speak the same Language~

~I keep my hand over my heart
to keep my feelings inside
and if they ever were to fall
let my hand be the first to handle them
for what God has placed firmly
in my chest to beat the Life in Me
Let not another hand dismantle it~

~I noticed my eyes were only used as a reflection
to see yourself~

~Moments don't last forever
but you can find forever in a moment~

Excalibur

Excalibur

It has been said that "The pen is mightier than the sword." However Marcus Garvey stated that "The pen is mightier than the sword, but the tongue is mightier than them both put together." The book of Hebrews 4:12 says "For the word of God is alive and exerts power and is sharper than any two edged sword and pierces even to the dividing of soul and spirit, and of joints and their marrow, and is able to discern thoughts and intentions of the heart."

There is no mistake in how alive I feel when either writing or performing my work. Words possess a power of knowledge that one needs to respect. One must control that power with having wisdom in the words that they profess. To the one who said "sticks and stones may break your bones but words may never hurt you" may have hurt more people than they intended to help. For words have created and destroyed. It has saved and it has killed. It has helped, motivated, hurt, hindered, and healed. So what words do you profess on the daily? How are you using your words? Choose them wisely before the power of what becomes of it, overcomes you!

From the start I wanted to write poetry to profess the truth. I wanted to give people what they deserved to know and heal people who were broken with lies. I wanted to tell peoples truths who couldn't profess their own. In doing so I had to reveal what hurt worse than the lies. I had to pierce them with the Good, Bad, and Ugly of the truth. I couldn't sugarcoat open wounds because it only leads to infection. I have to be raw, rare, and uncut because lives are at stake. Fortunately God has blessed me with the tools to attain this. He has gifted me with an Excalibur. Which is an artistic trinity that incorporates three utensils. Pen, microphone/platform, and the profession of truth; these three all put together to build a mighty two edged sword. With the aim to be sharp enough that it pierces even to the dividing of soul and spirit, and of joints and their marrow, and is able to discern thoughts and intentions of the heart. It is a representation of my imperfection. The irony that even in my wrongdoing I still fight for righteousness. It is a gift and a curse. A source of protection that has built me in stature and has structured my life. I would not be myself without it.

Passion, conviction, and repetition is the driving force that powers my sword in every battle. Each one very important in its own right. However repetition is one of the worlds greatest teachers. Repetition is one of the worlds greatest teachers. Repetition is one of the worlds greatest teachers! It is hard to forget if you constantly repeat it. My ambitions as a writer/poet is to imprint your soul with truths that will never leave your side, in a world that bombards you with lies.

<u>Equation</u>

Situation – Lie + Facts(Reason)= Truth
Situation – Lie + Facts(Reason)= Me
I spit Truth discombobulating speakers frequency
Frequently I'm the victim of slander
Diminishing Truths worth
Finally found a real nigga
But couldn't deal with her
Cuz Truth Hurts

Excalibur

I am Apollo with an Excalibur
a character that exceeds my caliber
a born sinner that can save souls
by removing sticks from stones
showing that my words can hurt worse than them
see the venom that is used to kill
will be the same poison I use to heal you with
poetry is my story
but without the throne and glory
I King authored it
created and conquered it
martyr of truth
so religiously I fought for it
murdering inc.
ever since I figured that Jah ruled
a gift given that I can't wait to show
off for him
relinquishing my evils into this inkwell
is my sacrificial offering
see my poetry is a beautifully written composition
to the ears of sound mind
music to a lost soul
it's a healing art
for the only rhythm I seek to speak to
is the beat of your heart
so either way my A Capella
is instrumental in healing your scars
imprint my spirit into your intellect until you swoon
serenading your forbidden fruit like an i tune
if art was war
then wordsmiths I'd goon
until my wrist get loose
with due time on my side
I'm never thirsty
I got my minutes made
it's like I'm Tupac with the juice

standing on the roof
but I'm no pushover I stay grounded
like a heavy weight
then turn around and defy gravity when I levitate
amazing is the outcome when I meditate
inhale until spoken words exhale
I self medicate
there is no subject I can't predicate
whether filtered or unedited
I make you respect it like it's etiquette
value morals until morals increase in volume
you're gonna need a cranium that's sound proof
in order to turn down what I've sound proofed
no matter how hard you may try
you may steer away
but you can't get around truth
because 51 out of 50
that 360 gonna hit you quickly
because that kin karma is more
than a hundred proof
it's a solution that's forever clear
a shot that is hard to swallow
a burn that will forever pierce your soul
and once you wake up from that knock out
trust me it will make a nigga want to stay woke
truth has always been a prophecy that is foretold
allowing me to be so far ahead of my time
that I admire my future in retrospect
for years I've been grinning at days like this
and no one knew what I was smiling at
see I gotta let my pen swim submarine deep in oceans
because if I let it run trains on your tracks
it's gonna make you wonder
yo, how she get away with murder
with locomotives
passion is a magic potion
conviction reinforces the spell you're under
let every illusion of figurative language allude

you to the truth
and she'll believe anything my pen tell her
like wallah, magic, Penn and Teller
there is a reason this knight shined
the stars were aligned
so that every mountain would be conquered by a goat
the only way to Top a Cap is to remove him
however your fear of this sign
only lets you see the world in horoscopes
if you want to be illuminated
put your eye in a diamond
for free is a mason
whose trade is building with units of various
artificial or natural products
so solid they call it a rock
let them be leaders
new world order will portray them
as Jehovah and Jesus
yet the King and Prince who were both whiteness
both died due to drugged incidents
scary how deep the Truth can get
in a world that is so photogenic
the Truth does more than paint the picture
the creator has allowed me to give the
photo synthesis
so I must live and die by my Excalibur
for I am fighting a war to show the magnitude
in which Truth exists

Who Am I

I cry with no tears
I bleed with no blood
I am afraid with no fear
I am happy with no good
I have sorrow with no pain
I am falling with total balance
I am enduring with no gain
I have competition with no challenge
I live with no heart
I breathe with no breath
I begin with no start
I vanish without death

Senses

Two eyes but our eyes are blind
So we won't pay attention
Two ears and we only hear
We don't take the chance to listen
Two nostrils only for sniffing
We're hardly ever breathing
Two hands not for building
they're only out for reaching
Two legs but we're never walking
Instead we keep them creeping
One mouth doing twice the talking
But neither word is for teaching

Out My Window

What I see out my window
I cannot say
for I see something different
everyday
I see young steppers on the street
using their feet to step to the beat
I see people being mislead
children needing education in their head
out my window I see children playing basketball
and girls playing with baby dolls
I see families having cookouts
and boys coming outside with their blowouts
this is what I see out my window

Life

Independent parents toiling
young black kids who mothers are spoiling
frustrating workdays, weeks, months, and years
pregnant adolescents whose mothers cry tears
money the cruelty of all peoples lives
the reason we got welfare and living in strife
racism the one thing that separates us all
the thing that's been going on for years
so why do you seem appalled
struggling the one thing that black people do best
but this is not what I or you say
it's what the media wants to stress
discipline something that our young people today lack
when are our parents going to keep them in tack
temptation the persuasive tactic that gets us to do wrong
even though we know we should have just moved along
Relationships something that never lasts long
because of bunch of he say she say
then you realize you both were wrong

although my life feels like I'm done
as my years go on
I assure myself that there's more to come
and even though at times you feel stabbed in the back with a knife
you may have to understand that this is life

Right is Wrong, Wrong is Right

To do right is wrong, and to do wrong is right
because I cannot walk away from ignorance
but in ignorance I can fight
to be a hypocrite is good
to be a liar is better
but to tell the truth they call out "behead her!"
I cannot die a lawyer, a doctor, or a professor
but I can die a thug, thief, drug dealer that's better
to be put in jail without bail is how one should strive
but to be successful in life the right way you are deprived
to lose your virginity at the age of 14 is the best way to be
but to keep it for that special one you are the joke of the streets
to reach a goal no one can reach, you are not a winner,
and to kill a creation of God you are not a sinner
because to do wrong is right, and to do right is wrong
though I never intended life to be this way,
I guess I knew it all along

No One Knows Me

You'll never know me
you'll never understand my tears
or my cries, or the reason for my lies
you wouldn't understand me
even if you were me
even if my thoughts were inside your head
even if you lived my life
you wouldn't understand why I've cried some nights
why those days I smiled
one can never figure me out
why I write the way I do
why I say what I say
why I act this way
NO ONE UNDERSTANDS ME
Why one minute I'm happy
and the next minute I'm not
why I can seem like I'm so full of life
and the next minute it is as if I'm going to die
why?
Why don't you know me
why don't I like what I use to like and vice versa
I use to love you now I curse you
no one knows me and they never will
even after my last breath
they wouldn't even know why I died
because society is so blind
I change as bluntly as the seasons
I find out more as life proceeds
and my thoughts are always going to change
but my name will always be the same
but you'll never know me
even if I told you myself
there is not one word to explain me
so why ask someone else?

Blinded

Crying, sighing, dying
in the most intimate part
of your body the heart
torn apart
because society has left you in the dark
born depraved
not knowing color, sex or age
bursting out in rage
because it was I when they talked
about the bird locked in a cage
will they let me go
will they let me free to show
this glow
that's inside of me but no one knows
or do they know
and it was just me that couldn't believe
that I could succeed
if I took care of what I need
to make me become a blessed seed
that way I could praise
while I raise my hand
and live my life under the man
and resurrect my game plan
to be the best that I can
and become the star not the fan
and to fully express who I am
as I unwrap this blindfold
to only behold
this ravishing image of God as I was told
to finally see this reflection in the mirror
I can see life a little more clearer
I can see the end drawing nearer
once was blind I opened my eyes
and I still can't fully see
but I'm discovering the way of life
and the way of me

I tried hard to see it
and I tried to find it
but it wasn't until they removed the covering
from my eyes to realize
that I had been blinded

Temptation

I have a sensation knocking on my door
and it hurts so bad he makes me sore
sometimes he's a foe sometimes a friend
that's why I'm contemplating if I should let him in
he sets my soul on fire
not a burning pain but a burning desire
Sometimes he controls your actions and emotions
takes so long he moves in slow motion
you know he's wrong, but you think he's right
got you thinking so much you can't fall asleep at night
see knocking on my door is a sensation
it's not pain, or love, his name is
Temptation

So called Woman

Oh so your a woman now
head above the clouds
cause you got a little body now
hands on your hip, head swinging from side to side
now don't you think that you're on cloud nine
yeah still living with your mother
intimidated by the world
and you're a real woman
how about a little girl
looking in my eyes and a real woman is what you're implying
talk about little battles
but in wars never fighting

think you're a big woman cause you mess with big men
and they only give you what you plan to give them
oh so you're a real woman
or just matured a lot quicker
go to the club and the first thing you drink is liquor
now you're all messed up and your mind has detoured
now your feeling things you never felt before
then before you know it
you're living in a world of Tina vs. Ike
but you're a real woman...
Sike!

Isolate

Take me away from the world and let me think
put me in solitude and let all those who say they need me wait
let me be alone and put outside the world
I want to go back to the stages of a lonely little girl
take me away from those I love
to see if I will miss them
take me away from God
let me see if I am really a Christian
take me away from me and let me witness my own fate
let me see my own life and witness my own mistakes
put me to the point where I can see what God sees
and maybe just maybe it'll make it easier on me

In My Body

In my mouth are the lies
and the truth is in my eyes
and others brutality is in my fists
and from between my thighs is a gift
on my chest lie two barriers
and my stomach is the carrier
on my skin is the brutality that others have given me
and in my heart are my past and present feelings
what keeps me straight is my spine
and every thought is in my mind
in my soul lives my life
and in my blood is red wine
I know that this doesn't define me
but in my body lies a story

I Never Knew

I never knew the things you went through
and when I found out I couldn't believe it was you
I never knew that life was this hard
and everywhere I go I have to keep up my guard
I never knew that you felt this way
why didn't you just tell me
I never knew that the streets were this deep
and that it's all about knowledge and deceit
there are a lot of things that I never knew
and it kind of made me feel slow
but maybe the things I never knew
I wasn't suppose to know

Da Truth

The truth is my life
from each happy day to the trouble and strife
the truth is in my eyes
look deep within you can see the truth is never disguised
the truth is in each poem, sentence, word, and line
the truth is within every rhyme
the truth is in my game
because every emotion comes out when I play
and the truth is what I write, say, and do
the truth is who I be
yes I fantasize but I don't live in fantasy
Da Truth is ME!

Ever Feel

Did you ever feel like each day was your last
and that you don't live for the future but the present and past
have you ever felt like all eyes were on you
especially when you're doing things you wasn't suppose to
or have you felt like your life is a dream and you don't exist
and something so good to you was someone else's wish
have you ever felt like everyone is against you
and your friends weren't really your friends
and your family was a front too
and did you ever feel like giving up on life itself
you're so tired of your story it's boring
so you put your book back on the shelf
or have you ever felt so sorry for yourself
but when you notice others doing worse
you feel sorry for not feeling sorry for someone else
did you ever feel so happy that nothing could mess up your day
but then there's that something that takes your joy away
and did you ever feel like the world was on your shoulders
because you have no life so you deal with the problems of others
or have you ever felt like no one loves you

and they only pretend that they care because they have to
have you ever felt a song that just explained your joy or pain
and you just feel relieved because another feels the same
were you ever feeling jealous that the thought of it was strenuous
but you couldn't help the feeling because the feeling was envious
and did you ever feel that you weren't you
 you're trapped in someone else's body doing what you really didn't
want to
did you ever feel a touch that really wasn't there
and the feeling felt good but the thought made you scared
did you ever feel so hurt that your breath was gone
but that's just the beginning and the hurt has yet to begun
just have you ever felt the feelings that I feel
but more importantly was the feeling real

Unexplainable

Unexplainable
the way we lead our lives
the reasons why we die
the tears that fall from our eyes
Unexplainable
the unlearned lessons
the unread messages
I just got an answer yet I still have a question
Unexplainable
life, liberty, and the pursuit of happiness
yet we're not equal
I'm a person but not considered apart of the people
everyone's after me yet I'm the weapon that's lethal
Unexplainable
so many rich and even more poor
I look for an entrance but they always shut the door
America wants to save more lives
so what's the death penalty for
Unexplainable
the truth that are found in lies

the good behind the crimes
the question why
Unexplainable
the day and the night
the pain and the strife
Unexplainable
life!

When I Try

When I try to do right
it seems like the world wants me to do wrong
I try to sing
but I can't find a song
I try to work
but I can't get a job
I try to go to school
and it seems like it's only me they're testing
I try to worry about myself
but everything else is so stressing
when I try to love
they don't love back
and when I try to walk away
I still get attacked
when I try to be apart of the solution
I'm still apart of the problem
I try to be in the light
and I still find myself in the darkness
but when I give up people wonder why
cause when I try
the only ones that care are
me, myself, and I

My Mind

My mind wanders
and I can't help but to ponder
about the things I go through
for me it seems like so much but for others it's few
I sit and think about future, present, and past
think about death, I wonder how long it will last
I think and I worry about others
friends, family, mothers, fathers, sisters, and brothers
think about certain situations
that led to so much stress and complications
I wonder about the things I don't understand
I wonder about far away places and distant lands
I think about how people would react if I died
would they come to see me if I'm dead or will they cry
I think about losing someone dear to me
and how would I deal with the pain eternally
but as my mind wanders
I ponder about things that affect me

Life is not a Game

Life is not a game that is the name of this poem
you don't get no points for the way you live on
you can't depict your life because of the hand you're dealt
because your hand can spell out poverty
then you're living in wealth
life leaves you with no chances and time always goes on
and ones destination is never fully controlled
every challenge is not guaranteed a win or a lose
and sometimes the path you walk is not the one you choose
life is about survival and life is about adjusting to change
but never should it be written that life is a game

The Beast

I've been broken, beaten, bruised
left lonely and confused
I have felt useless and used
and my privacy has been invaded
and my past I've hated it
looking back at my life it wasn't good
dealing with issues I didn't know I could
especially at my age
I was crying for days
going through too many things
I had to deal with fist fight
and he the beast trying to claim my mom as a slave
never considered her as wife
I remember going to school scared
thinking of what could've happened when I wasn't there
will she live again or has she died
overwhelmed with happiness after school when I see her eyes
she survived
from this beast that I could see through
but she was too blind
to realize that she was royalty
being controlled by a swine

Victim Woman

I saw her just like I seen many other women
Stuck behind four walls as if it were a prison
Because this man raised his hand
And on your knees you landed
And by bruises you were branded
His property
And he was treated like royalty
But less than a peasant is what he is naturally
Yes I watched you
Sitting in the corner of your room
Forced to love a man who didn't love you
and for so many years
You asked yourself what should I do
It seemed as if you had no clue
As if leaving this man would not make your life improve
So you stayed with the cruel
Over him he made you drool
In public you were made the fool
Yes woman you are the victim
Of a man who made promises he couldn't keep
Who's actions meant more than his words
Because no matter how many times he said he would stop
He would go out and creep
And come back so your face he could beat
And then you would run out and call the police
And he would chase after
As if he didn't want you to leave
But little did you know this man had more tricks up his sleeve
He would get on his knees
Beg you please
for right now he would
Treat you like a queen
He would tell you everything that you wanna hear
Like how he's always gonna be there
And how he never meant it, to put his hands on you
Baby I never meant to hurt you

He explains how he's been going through things
He hugs and kisses you
Telling you that things are gonna change
He grabs your hand and offers you a ring
He whispers in your ear how much joy he could bring
He even uses the faces of his kids
And says without them how he can't live
While they're sitting there crying screaming
Mommy don't leave daddy
And he uses that to say let's become a family
He gets to you good enough before the cops come
So when they ask you what's you going on
You explain that you have made a mistake
As you apologize for the call
You fall into the arms of the snake
That food he fed you must've been great
Because you ate
All the crap off his plate
And the whole time y'all walking home
He's deciding your fate
Saying let's make up with love
And you agree unconscious to the rape
and in that moment of time
all of you is what he takes
So once again you're behind bars
A body full of scars
weeks of broken jaws
a life full of flaws
But woman there is a better life that you can be living
So pack your bags and get your children
Because this man is not worth the tears
that your eyes have been dripping
I know inside you were dying
But it's time to live again
Time to show this sorry excuse for a man
That you cannot be with him
And if he ever raises his hand up to you again
That's when you cock back and put this man in his place

And if he gets too close you hit him in the face
Or in that spot below the waist
You give him what you once had to take
Tell him don't come ten miles near you or your kids
because there is a life that you have a life to live
That does not involve him or his sins
Make it clear the first time and don't tell him twice
And if he gets close again threaten his life
Make him see that you will kill him
Because woman that's what it takes
To not become a man's victim

Internal Conflicts

Overwhelmed emotions that I hide
all contradicting themselves inside
scared to love because love may be deceiving
but yet love is what I'm seeking
waiting to enjoy pleasure because I want to be pleased
but please take heed
for I know within me can be embedded a seed
which is a blessing
but a blessing right now that I don't need
or can I be infected with a disease
could it be the death of AIDS
or just the beginning HIV
wanting to trust
but wondering if the person is worth being trusted
wondering if I will reach my dream
or let my reality be
that I can't touch it
wanting to do right but I keep doing wrong
hoping God will listen to my same sad sorry song
knowing I need to change
because judgment may take place tomorrow
these are the internal conflicts
that bring so much grief and everlasting sorrow

or is it those that within you hold
when you really want to let go
but you don't want to break up the house
that was never your home
so you don't let go
and you let them keep their little humble abode
though inside you roam
within a world you call your own
and you say to yourself I'm going to do it
when you know you won't
so on the inside how does one cope
when the world outside leaves you with no hope

A Cry For Help

Mama, I stayed out all night,
you know I might have sinned
and you're steady looking at me with same sad grin
see daddy, you know I was in a fight at school
and all you wanna know is
"did you win cause I didn't raise no fool"
we sit and we wonder what is life supposed to be
and we ain't get real answers just a lot of wannabes
you tell me life is a bag of chips
so why do I continue to slip
you know I tell you everyday what I've done wrong
and you continue to ignore me and
not have clue of what's going on
do you want to know something?
I haven't cried a tear even when grandma died
let me tell you why
because I have continued to cry for help
but no one could hear my yelp
see I have continued to cry and plea
but no one would answer me
see that's why I will not say one word
because of my heart it burns

that's why I shall not shed one tear
because of no love and fear
that's why I continue to stay down
because no one has offered to uplift me
and get me off the ground
that's why I don't want to go on
because of my life it's torn
maybe I don't know how to cry anymore
because I'm all cried out and life is no more
though I have continued to cry for help
but no one could hear my yelp
see I have continued to cry and plea
but no one would answer me
then I woke up from a nightmare
and knew someone cared
that's how my whole nightmare felt
just a cry for help

Testers

People, who push you to the limit
you tell them to mind their business but they always
find a way to get in it
instigators, the ones who try to push your friends away
you try to ignore them but in your face they'll always stay
bullies these are the people who try to put you down
little do they know how you can really throw down
players the ones who mess with you, your best friends, and your favorite
cousin from the west
these are the people who will put you to the test
haters, people who don't have one good word to say
these are the testers of our past, future, and our present day
misery, the one who loves company
they want you to go down because their lives are crummy
while in this world you will find no confessors,
just the instigators, bullies, haters,
but I label them testers

I Cry

I cry when my heart is filled with sorrow
when I open my eyes and it feels like there's no tomorrow
I cry when I feel regret
of me and my family not being confederate
I cry when I think of my mother
and it hurts me to death when we don't cooperate together
I cry when I don't past the test
the test that God has given me
so my soul can be put to rest
I cry when people die for no reason
but that's what we get for Adam and Eve eating the fruit
in the garden of Eden
I cry when I'm happy and free
why?
Because this is just how I am this is just me
so don't tell me to dry my eyes
instead I'd rather cry

Living a Lie

Living a lie is like living in
an abode that they call house
but yet it's not my home
because there does not exist my soul
it's just a place to lay my head
and to keep me a little warm
yet the hearts there are cold
living a lie is like carrying a load
that is hard to hold
and you live like a coward
because only the truth is bold
living a lie is like living in another
persons dreams
where you do not succeed because
it's not your fantasy
living a lie is making tomorrow
harder than it needs to be
it's only living in truth that makes life
worth living

Imperfect Child

Lessons are taught to him
that he has not learned
goodness is what keeps him happy
but sometimes evilness is what he yearns
knowing what you say is right
but he still becomes more stubborn
he tries to calm down
but it's out of spite when he gets wild
he gives you spicy
when you asked for mild
he wants to turn the world right side up
but he keeps turning the world upside down
he wants to light up the sky with a smile

but all he can do is frown
he wants to be apart of the solution
but he's constantly a problem
once he found his way
and just as easily he lost it
he tries to reach for the sky
but he still falls short
as he tries to excel
in both academics and sport
but it seems like the devil
always finds a way
to make this child
apart of his company
he will never always be pure
but he can always be foul
he can learn many things
but that doesn't mean he will understand
how to apply them now
and it's all because man and woman
weren't perfect
so why expect a Perfect Child

My Life Is On The Line

It was senior farewell
and I performed where do I go from here
and I thought many had listened and enjoyed the words
but never did I think
anyone would approach me in tears
like this one lady did
as she came to me arms open and she wept
gave me the tightest hug
saying "you don't even know what you've done"
wiped her tears and left
and just like that one
there are other stories that bother me
like after speaking my Jesus piece
and an older lady walks up to me and says "because of you
now I can die in peace"
or even when performing at this place that I did not intend to be
and this young man walks up to me
and says "because of you I want to write poetry"
and he didn't even know me
none of them did
and it's amazing how I gave one lady the
comfort to die in peace
but see I don't want to stop until I give someone a reason to live
or even the courage to change
these stories explain how my want to sleep
and my urge to write fight at night
because I gotta write
I have to write
because these lines are not just my life
and sometimes I don't even think you take me seriously
it's like I write for it not to be read
or I speak for no one to hear me
but if you did
you would understand that this is more than poetry
this is my destiny my purpose
and I know because sometimes when writing

I still get nervous
because I never know what the next verse is
until it comes
I got 99 problems and this pen ain't one
it's like pieces of perfection when a poem is done
man I gotta write
I have to write
because these lines are not just my life
but they are never ending stories
of the ones who wrote before me
and the ones who will come after
sometimes you don't even have to read in between the lines
you can plainly see how each poem is a chapter
it's amazing how with one word
your emotion can be captured
how with one word you can trigger
your brain to formulate picture
causing flashbacks of laughter, cries,
happy times, rage and even signs of vigor
you can't tell me that this here
is just mere talent entertainment
no see this here is bigger
it's so much bigger than you and me
because there is someone out there right now
who needs a poet to tell their story
who needs a poet for motivation, fulfillment, closure
who needs a poet to give them clearance
and show them the bridge to go over
or maybe just a helping
these poetic lines give breath to a chest compressed
for there is comfort when someone else understands
so do you see my attachment
or better yet my alliance
my life is on the line
for if the day comes that I go silent
or I never let my pen leak ink
and I discontinued my writing
then I would have reneged upon my blessings

for I have denied access of an outlet
for an inspired soul to triumph
so when the urge of my fingertips grip pen
I shall deny my writing
and when a venue seeks for me to speak
I will not remain quiet
there is a true conviction in my addiction
there is no way to stop me
I will not go down this time
please understand that my life is on the line
for this here I will fight
because I got to write
I have to write
because these lines are not just my life

~I am a work of art
who works my art
to only Master Peace~

Just Human

I write with the hand of God
That is held by the arm of a Man
Remember, understand
I am just human (2x)
But some don't understand
For they only view my blessing
Forgetting my structure is that of a human
Who struggles with flaws and falls due to imperfection
Scarred with this beautiful infection
Of a gift and a curse
And it hurts to know that harsh judgment lurks
Where God's wonders work
I mean what kind of world is this to live through
That's why I gotta keep my vision peripheral
Make sure my soul stays spiritual

See it's all for the mental
Whether I'm spitting it raw
Or giving you written material
Gotta remember to keep my head up in deep water
See my empathy is more than feeling you
See I've been through those days
Where my breakfast, lunch, and dinner was cereal
And the struggle I'm still living
When the only real dinner I get is on thanksgiving
And thoughtful people seem to only think about me on Christmas
Or my birthday which is the worst day
Tryna buy me a drink at the bar nigga
Yesterday I was thirsty
But my thirst has been quenched
And my bill money has been spent
So that means my pockets are full of lint
But my soul stays rich
Because my mind makes more than cents
See I got a few dollars in my scholar
My diploma is my presence
Graduated top of my class soul survivor
The truth is I'm cool
But this poetic flow is on fire
Ignited by pain, passion, rage,
And something higher
They say good things forget where they came
Man I'm from the home of the wire
I said I write with the hand of God
That is held by the arm of a Man
Remember, understand
I am just human
See I'm born sinner still saint
I've been rewarded because I've pulled my weight
See I'm on the right road
But there's been days where I've switched lanes
Sidetracked, for the strength thereof that I lacked
Let the temporary pleasure of insecure happiness
Beat me in combat

But despite the fallback
I always fought back
Listened to God and tried not to talk back
Shhhhhhh
And then I just let him right my ways
And then I just let him write my ways
So I close my eyes let fingertips grip pen
And I write for days
Yes I write for days
Something so sick
That HIV and AIDS died because they got a whiff of it
crackheads went to rehab because they stop itching
And Bush got re elected, apologized to all niggas
And got some sense in him
Said equal opportunity For All
And Africans got rich again
But this is only something Gods gift can give
To write this way is a gift to men
To get a glimpse of what perfection is
But please don't view me as the perfectionist
I just try inspire with every chance I get
With every move I make
And with every poem I spit
I said I write with the hand of God
That is held by the arm of a Man
Remember, understand
I am just Human

Ghetto Princess

See she had no big house or picket fences
This is ghetto living
Daddy had another home
Mom was just a mistress
School of hard knocks under no supervision
Math wasn't a subject
It was more like a decision
Spreading her legs was her division
And if she multiplied before 18
She ends up a statistic
But don't get it twisted
Voice of a songbird
Shorty she was gifted
Delectable in every way
but malice was her nutrition
Only thing cooking was the rock up in the kitchen
So down to earth she needed something to keep her lifted
Zoned out she like being past the point of pretending
Broken homes turning into different dimensions
It was non violent and no drama from moms bitching
Said she wouldn't get carried away
But kept drifting
In a zone she ain't never wanna leave
So she went to sleep to keep her eyes on her dreams
In hopes she'll never miss it
A shame that she will never live it
People got me reminiscing
Ghetto love for my Ghetto princess

My Eye is on the Barrel

He said I bang because no one loves me
I slang because nothing in life is free
he said my eye is on the barrel
because I know it watches me
see crime pays when you're hungry
gotta get that bread, lettuce, and cheese
but unfortunately in these streets
no sandwich is complete without the beef
they said healthy is a vegan
but my only green thumb
is from the root of all evil
see if I ruled I'd change projects to villages
overdose on love
and bring back the barter system
see it all starts with a change in midset
because if only
U aNd I Thought of Each other Daily
our Consciouses would be UNITED

Baltimore

I hate but I love this jungle
Hear sirens when barrel echoes
Non violent, Please They'll Malcolm X you
On the Blvd. Of MLK see here ain't no one special
So be careful when darkness falls
Close your windows and lock your doors
Because they're taking what they can't afford
These niggas be breaking laws when they get bored
It's on
Like protection that you must hold
Whether it's waist side or pants low
Because if you get caught with your eyes closed
Catch that A.I. Die Slow
You know
See around here it's hustlers harvest

And the target is Lexington market
When you're fiending for a fixing from the kitchen
Whether it's rocks or it's chicken
Ham hocks or pot you can get it
Serve you up with pipes or the dishes
See every customer gets addicted
You living day by day
We surviving minute by minute
To America we're a menace
We should be in the book of Guinness
And this is only the beginning
And niggas scared for me to finish like Truth quit it
But they need to be reminded
Because the industry keep forgetting
That we're the ones that kicked the dirt up out the earth
And gave birth to a Ruff Ryder
We the ones robbing banks like Jada and still surviving
We are the ones banging shots and never missing
Like Sam Cassel and Juan Dixon
Always hitting like 92q on your stereo
Banging Tony Braxton and Mario
This area yo is too live
We taught Ginuwine how to ride
We are the rose that grew from concrete
That's the beauty of these streets
See we are never giving up
So don't worry about who shot ya
We'll just Tupac ya
And tell you Keep your Head up
And if you don't believe me just watch us on TV
they mock our strut, they like our swag
And our build is too tough
Even Jay-Z wanna go harder than us!

Addicted

Yea I'm addicted
And I ain't afraid to say it
See I'll tell you point blank
That I sniff black words off white pages
You got a poetry venue
I'm scratching myself near stages
I can't stop shaking
Body steady aching
For that profound sound of poetry
Please inject that sweet taste of
Metaphors, ideas, alliteration, proverbs, and similes
Right into me
I fiend for the thought of you having the thought
To express your thought on the Mic
So if you're scared to recite or your produce gets low
Just pass me the Mic and I'll inhale what I blow
That's right
I get high off my own supply
I'll make my own adrenaline rush
See I'm so addicted that too much is never enough
And enough is never reached
See I've gotten so high that I reached peaks peak
And broken through
And I'm a pro at this
So imagine what one hit will do to you
I mean this stuff ain't no joke
I seen one dude try to take a hit on the mic and choked
Tell me if you're ready
Tell me if you're ready to be put in the position
Where atheist became Christian
Where the key was found to unlock the door to your prison
Where the water you could barely keep your head above
Became water you could swim in
This is my addiction
I'm addicted to the change of perspective
The life lesson

The mirror that made me see my own reflection
I'm addicted to words played to perfection
Ask my doctor if you need someone to cosign
See I got doctor reports that say
I have Truth flowing through my veins
And faith in my bloodlines
And knowledge that pierces my soul
I've witness this stuff turn a half man whole
So believe me when I tell you I'm a fiend and I'm picky
Especially when it comes to that sticky icky
So for all you pushers out there I need y'all to get focused
Because whether written or spoken I need my poetry potent
Something that's gonna keep my eyes open
And give me that sensation that poetry can only make me get
Somebody light this mic
I need another hit

Knowledge

Knowledge
a gift and a curse
to know or not to know which is worst
for knowledge equates power
but are you wise enough to control it
are you intelligent enough to decipher
when the worth of knowledge
is not worth knowing
can you be mature enough to accept
the fact that true knowledge is common sense
can you accept the fact
that innocence is ignorance
and ignorance is bliss

Vanity

I was taught to never let your left hand
know what you're right hand is doing
no need to brag about the people I've uplifted
or the goals that I'm pursuing
just know that when I respond
that I'm just cooling
when they ask me how I'm doing
it's due to my planted seeds turned trees
chilling all shade no tea
because a hydrated soul
is never thirsty
for peace, love, life and prosperity
are blessings best enjoyed
silently

Gone

I want to die in peace
I want to go not knowing
I am leaving
I ask Jehovah to please take me
while I'm sleeping
dreaming of a perfect evening
with all the ones I love
for your paradise will never
be apart of my future
so I beg for mercy upon
my soul
for if my existence should perish
please let me go
not knowing I am leaving
Jehovah please take me
while I'm sleeping
dreaming of a perfect evening
with all the ones I love

~God told me to
treat the stage like it's My jungle gym
only spit Monkey bars
Guaranteed they'll hang on your every word, word
He told me
To treat the stage like it's my jungle gym
Only spit Monkey bars
Guaranteed they'll hang on your every word, word, word...~

Poetic Bars

These are poetic bars
No punchlines
Just prophetic sparring
Outside the ring
No need for battling
But just in case you wanna battle me
Understand that I'm lethal
And with no Vaseline
You'll get fucked with that ether
So until you boys grow up
On that ass I'll be priesting
Preaching how the streets are deceiving
Leaving these Chuckys cheesing
But they'll never be a token child
Playing this game will never give you
Tickets to a way out
Because once you're in
It's difficult to change routes
Keep it 100 with ugly truths
Like I'm a bastard child
Unplanned but on purpose nigga
So how you like me now
See I'm certified 100 new millennium Benjamin
They call me blue bucks
Get more heads under sheets than the Klu Klux
I guess that's why they call me a loose leaf

See I'm too nuts for y'all to do me
See I been claustrophobic ever since I came out the closet
Too open minded for boxes
No rotation in my circle that makes me nauseous
See we stand still and let the world revolve around us
You should take your time and study me
Like the Bible the Odyssey and Iliad
In order to get schooled by me you need prerequisites
See I'm not an intellectual poet
I'm an intellect with common sense
And there's no way to make this long story short
The way I be stroking with my penmanship
Flow so lyrically retarded that if my tongue could dance
It would moonwalk forward
Turn bars into bricks
To seperate from all the brain cells I done built
I swear it's levels to this Tetris kid
Flow so heavy that I Always keep a Maxi pad
To absorb all of the seepage
But you niggas is spotting you barely leaking
Ultra thin with your lines boy that niggas is barely feeling it
Provoke a conscious with your content nigga
Point Blank Period!
See you want the point but you
Keep starring at the top of the pyramid
But I'm within the walls among the symbols
And the hieroglyphs
I'm fresh and my flow clean
Like oxy to you morons
I tell the truth like equal
Is the right to two wrongs
Flow foreign so comprehension
May require Rosetta stone
To speak the tongue of a third eye
Live and die by the sword like a samurai
I swear the way the truth hurts
You would've of thought I was a bad guy
But I'm really too nice with it If you thought I was coldhearted

It's really that I'm anemic and my bloods thinning
See it's a generational trait
Substituting water for your bloodline
Dealing with your demons
Until the devil ain't so bad that dude is alright
I said dealing with your demons until the devil
Ain't so bad that dude is alright
They say Truth you feeling yourself
You cocky even
And I said yea but not for no arrogant reasons
So I'm a keep feeling myself until I masturbate
Masterpieces...
Of words God made me a master Genius!

~What kind of Poet are you
For I am a
Prophet Orally Expressing Testimonies
so are you a
Person Over Exaggerating Truths
or are you
Purposely Oppressing Everyone's Thoughts
What kind of Poet are you?~

~I rewrite the lessons that I've learned
while not listening to what God has already taught me~

~I wish I didn't know the Truth
they say God only takes care of babies and fools
and I wish I didn't know the Truth
sometimes I'd rather be a fool than responsible~

~My deepest thoughts are the ones
with no answers, the ones with no reason
for true depth is a free fall with no ending
My deepest writing is an unfinished sentence
and my deepest thought is unwritten~

~ They love that I'm Da Truth
but they hate that I'm Honest~

~If when you speak and people listen
you have been blessed to save lives~

~Being reminded that someone has been through
worse never changes the fact that your pain still hurts~

~I do not fear who I am
I decided to protect all that I have~

~Someday there won't be a One day to look forward to~

~Only the feeble minded would suggest
that one slave is greater than the other.
A wise man would suggest that neither is great without freedom~

~Life is a Teacher
there is a reason
it takes the eye of an owl
and the slickness of a snake
to prey upon a rat
Therefore be a student of reason
listen to your Teacher~

Controversy

Controversy

Where there is Truth, there are lies, and there are opinions. In turn this breeds controversy. The very foundation in which the judicial system was built. Trying to find the truth/resolution so that justice will prevail. Knowing this I have to ask myself. What is the truth about pigment being the determining factor of one person being greater than another? What is the truth about unrighteous acts being just? What is the truth about governments who support unrighteousness? Have we forgotten what righteousness is? It is the act of being righteous, virtuous, just, upright, honest, good, fair, and morally right!

Therefore I see no good in hate unless you are hating what is evil. I see no honor or equality in casting stones when your glass house is submerged in the waters of your own sins. I find no virtue in making a mockery of those who are not like me or you. I see no justice in the killing of innocent lives. I see nothing morally right about the sex, money and drugs that run this system. Righteous ways should be the aim right?

So when you ask me about color as it pertains to people. I will sound off my agony and frustration but I will ultimately reply that "No one asks a star what color it is when it shines." To all reading this I just want to see you for the star you are. Let your spirit shine so bright that I see no color at all. And if I ever get close enough to see your hue in which you shine. For me it will only add to your awe. It is important to remember that no matter what color you are, every person is not your friend or your enemy.

When you ask me my opinion on this system of things. I will simply say "if you ain't got dollars than you can't get change." Most importantly I will provide them with a truth that hits a bit harder, "A government without God is manslaughter."

When you ask about my belief system. I will proudly say "I am Gods creation, nothing short of great yet nowhere near greater than the one who created me." I am nothing without the one who causes to become, Jehovah God. For he has instilled in me what righteousness is. He is the reason that the good in me prevails. The righteousness in me has been guided by what many call "The Good Book" or His word the bible. I perceive this blessing as nothing short of amazing. Just from a literary standpoint it transcends over all literary works. It is no doubt a work of art to admire and learn from. As stated before he is the one who has awarded me with my Excalibur, my sword. For you can't spell sword without putting the word in it. The word of God of course!

World Peace

If there was world peace suffering would end
all would be united and colors would blend
there would be no pain, crying nor sorrow
people wouldn't die today but forever see tomorrow
if there was world peace violence would cease
and there would be food, clothing, and shelter for everyone at least
if there was world peace everyone would get along
there would be no fighting over what's right or wrong
if there was world peace
there would be no more prejudice and segregation
because this world would work as one nation
for it is of one creation

The World

As I wander in this world day by day
I ask myself how can I live in such a pitiful place
where babies become disposable and thrown into lakes
and where people are making careless mistakes
this world use to have morals everyone understood
but who can understand now when you're living in the hood
see today everyone is worried about
that bling bling
and those platinum mouths
but who can understand true words
when our mouths are foul
all I'm saying is that this world has changed
and all our yester years will never be the same

United

United is when many come together as one
and they don't fuss or fight instead they have fun
united is when each color can stand face to face
and become one the human race
united is when each race can say to each other
she's my sister and he's my brother
despite the color
united is when no one will be alone
because there's one of your brothers or sisters
providing a home
that you can sleep in and halfway own
united is when many becomes one
and this way is much more fun

Death Penalty

A sinner decides the death of a sinner
that's what the death penalty does
it's the most hypocritical killer that ever was
trying to save more lives
but death is their wish
and the best thing about it
is that blacks are at the top of the list
and the death penalty
always finds the best kinds
as I recall
it's always the ones who don't commit the crime
is the government blind
giving the death penalty
a responsibility
that is not yours or mines
but the one above
how can we live peacefully
under a law of death
when we are taught to live and love

<u>Why?</u>

Why is the grass so green
 and why do my parents scream
why is the sky and ocean blue
and where did we come from
yes, me and you
why do we all have problems
and why can't we solve them
why are there people on the street
and why doesn't the government help
them get back on their feet
why is there black on black violence
and why do we live in silence
why was there world war 1 and 2
and how did many become few?

The New and Old World

It started in 1914 when world war 1 began
was it a trend
changes the paces of violence
no one listens to silence
everyone wants to dominate
but not concentrate
because we feel there's no time to think
these people don't defuse
instead they defy
and it's making all the little children cry
why because people seem to cease to believe
that diseases are coming back terribly
everyone scared for their lives
because there is nowhere to turn to
or anywhere to hide
because there are weapons on each corner of our eyes
everyone on their knees begging please
trying to get oxygen from the trees
people trying to find answers to whole lot of questions
but we're only getting guesses
now will this worldly trend ever end
what do you think

Tears of Life

My people are crying
but their cries are silent
it seems like no one hears them but I
so I just keep on writing
I said my people are crying
so my pen keeps bleeding
and as blood roles down this page
it forms words for the weeping
I said my people are crying
because its answers they're seeking
holding fast to the week days
because they might not make it to weekends
and through the cracks I see their eyes
they just keep on peeking
they're trying their best to find the light
but the crack is too small to see it
and because they can't see
they don't ever try to be it
these people never heard the words
if you believe then you can achieve it
so they walk this world hungry
and no one ever tries to feed them
and it doesn't get any better
because the media loves to tease them
showing them nothing but money and riches
everything from their dreams to their wishes
from ballers with fat pockets
to hoes giving out french kisses
I guess that's why on the streets
I always see my sisters steady looking for drug dealers
she never looks for anything different
and all the real men she dismisses
and whats funny about this situation
is that it's a big imitation of our TVs to our CDs
they're all procrastinating
quick to say we're leaders

but when push comes to shove we follow
I'm searching for true hearts
but the hearts I find are hollow
we are blind to the reality of how we live
but the life of a superstar is vivid
if life is a big imitation then the question becomes
how are we really suppose to live it
see I'm putting this out now because time is ticking
God promised us a paradise
so how long you think he's gonna let us live with the wicked
this thing right here is sickening
because we went from picking white cotton balls
to producing white pills and white powder
doing all the dirty work
giving white men all the power
ain't nothing change not even the time frame
we still live by minutes and hours
and what we do not a dag on thing
we just sit and wait for the fat lady to sing
and when she sung
down went the twin towers
now we represent our dead with teddy bears and flowers
so I pray in God's will that peace be still
but peace be steel and that's the will of the streets
see the streets never had its peace
but it always had its heat because a dogs gotta eat
see the streets are surrounded by dogs and chicken heads
see the dogs stay on the prowl only to get fed
and these chickens are only around to lay eggs
so these dogs use these chicks only to get fed
leaving chicks dead and her eggs unwatched
see we are the society of animals
and our so called trainers are the cops
if you haven't noticed we are only to speak on demand
told to sit or stand
and the force comes with a stick in their hand
man didn't know how the past was still in the palm of our hand
see we all cry for a piece of love,

a piece of joy, a piece of life
that's why I spit this piece to you
hoping these words go far beyond a poetry venue
but until they do I'm telling you that my people are crying
but their cries are silent
it seems like no one hears them but I so I just keep on writing
I said my people are crying so my pen keeps bleeding
and as blood roles down this page it forms words for the weeping
I said my people are crying
but tears no longer form
death is a celebration
my people no longer mourn
my man said he has joy for those who live not
and he mourns for those who live on
he said what's the point of fighting for life
when death is the norm
and who wants to live when families are torn
and there's no chance of hope
our life consists of running from reality,
responsibility, ourselves the cops
he said in life you get no chances no shots
he said the only shot you got is by the glock
and the only road we got is the block
and the block stays hot
so you tell me where's my spot
he said my only spot is with death
when I'm at rest and no burdens are on my chest
he said that's my true freedom
no more tests from the demons
I said my people are weeping because they are living in sin
steady living on hoop dreams ball never reaching the rim
united we never stood
divided that is why we fall
stay looking for imperfect, mortal leaders to do the governing job
when the only true governor is the
all powerful, immortal, Jehovah, and Jesus my Gods
my people are weeping
because it's answers they're seeking

we're living in the land of the demons
my people are tired of dreaming
my people are crying
we keep looking for bling
not realizing we're the diamonds
it's just that we're in the rough
believe me being this beautiful is tough
because true beauty goes through enough
but one day we will shine it takes time
my people are crying
but their cries are silent
it seems like no one hears them but I
so I just keep on writing
I said my people are crying
so my pen keeps bleeding
and as blood roles down this page it forms words for the weeping
I hope you listened with your heart
because this was more than just words I was speaking

Untitled

This poem is about you and me
The birds and the bees
Can't start my car because I lost my keys type of poem
See this poem is about the hypocritical
The average so I call them typical
Liars so they're political
This is about the people who give judgment
To my race the stereotypical
This is about the rich and the poor
The rejection letter on my front door
Us receiving so little when we only wanted more
This is the poem that relates to my sisters on welfare
Who still takes care of their kids when nobody else cares
Working so hard for the little bit of money just to get his fare
This is about friends turning to foes
And foes turning to friends
And the way one ends is a new way one begins
This poem is about the heartache, struggle, and pain
Going out of our way just to gain
The little bit of equality just to be judged the same
Ain't it a shame
How people work so hard just to get that high
And won't get a real job to save their lives
And just for some money they put their lives on the line
They don't worry about their life ahead
They're ready to commit the crime
This is about how my people just can't say no
For that dough, that puff, that hoe
But it's all they can say when they see five-O
Oh and lets not forget about the ones like me
Living in a fantasy
Waiting for the chance to be free
From all this violence and depression
Cruelty and deception
No answers a whole lot of questions
This is about how we sit through the stories

and never learn the lessons
This is about the men and women who make the babies
And how these men and women don't love but hate the babies
So foster care takes the babies
And they go to new homes
Where new men and women rape the babies
This poem is about how these babies grow up and become crazy
Or mentally disturbed
And now they smoke that herb
Just to forget about the times when they were hurt
Because it's either smoke that or to smoke themselves
Because we live in poverty not wealth
And the government won't help
They don't care about our health
And we don't care about where we go
When we die because we're already living in hell
See this poem is about where we are to start
And where we are to end
And where are we to go for our hearts to be mended
And where are we to go just to find that best friend
That will always be there when you need someone to listen
See this is a poem that could go on forever
It could talk about time
It could talk about the weather
It could talk about the times
That me and you were together
It could talk about success
It could talk about survival
But see this poem talks about so much
That it could only be called untitled

Reality

The reality is 4 kids in one bed
Laying from head to toe
All four kids wishing they could have a family
Like the Cosby show
The reality is the improvement of technology
Messed up the music industry
Cause common sense tells a black person to
Make their own CD
And charge someone less than they would usually
So we make it easier to get it
But society calls it bootlegging
The reality is, is that it's all about the hustle
And we wouldn't have to hustle
If we didn't have to struggle
But we've been struggling since the beginning
Since my day job, since my father packed and gone,
Since that cotton we was picking
See this is all reality ain't none of its fiction
It seems like it's so hard to get a college education
But so easy to get out of jail
See the reality is they make it hard to get money for books
But it's too easy to get money for bail
See the reality is that the government wants us to be poor
Every time they put an eviction notice on my front door
And raise everything more and more
And a sista like me gets tired of hearing
Have a nice day
When every year they wants to be raising the price for a bus pass
On the MTA
They wants to be taking most of my pay
Then they're ready to fire me
As soon as I ask for a raise on my salary
But what can I say
The reality is
Kids having kids
That's what it is

And it's these men
Just donating their seamen
When they're really boys trying to be men
They're looking for a girl to please them
And when you ask them why they reply
It feels good and that is their reason
See it's our own country that's committing the treason
Because instead of nurturing us with goods
Sex, drugs, and violence is what they feed them
The reality is men trying to deny his kids
Knowing that child has eyes just like his
So he chills with the mother for awhile
Just because of the child
But his frustration turns into domestic violence
But she says nothing her tears are so silent
I wish she would stop crying
And I wish he would start working
And stop flirting with chicken heads who are probably burning
See I'm not speaking statistics
I'm speaking the facts
Like how when we're broke we try to put other people's kids
On our income tax
And we say that we'll pay them back with some food stamps
And how mama always sent us to the store for those kool-aid packs
But that's all apart of being black
Or maybe just being poor
Because the reality is poor people have to improvise
Just to survive
Or just to get by in this day and time
So what must we do to succeed
Because the reality is no one is giving away anything for free
We have to work hard for what we need
See the reality is ain't nothing coming easy
And to get a man you have to dress Sleazy
But that's not reality
That's false advertisement that people need to stop believing
Because real men want real women
And want to have a hard time getting

What a real woman is capable of giving
See the reality is how each and every one of us is living
And every one of you could notice this reality too
If you just payed attention

Man Vs. Machine

Man vs. machine is like
who reigns supreme in life
rap & poetry speak life speak life
I said Man vs. machine is like
who reigns supreme in life
rap & poetry speak life speak life
imperfect creator creating perfect perpetrator
I guess us naturalist just can't get right
forget elders we flock to computers for insight
termination due to upgrade of creation
they said they're saving a price
I spit for intervention of invention
got me battling stripes
man this world is a stage
you can't refrain from the light
especially when your fate is in the hands
of a tracking device
and they equipped and ready
machinery getting heavy
they're prepared for the fight
and I ain't gonna die for nothing
Armageddon at the press of a button
no telling when nuclear war gonna ignite
so since they create with accuracy
we gotta be more than precise
it's time for the heist
so hit the backspace no time for rewrites
we got one life
rap & poetry at war with one mic
like man vs. machine is like

who reigns supreme in life
rap & poetry speak life speak life

Root of all Evil

I've been trying to get this paper
ever since I got laid off
my bills still gotta get paid off
hustling trying to scrape up this paper
it's time to get money I need to get money
for shopping sprees, gold, glitter & bliss
I wish
I need it for BGE, bad credit deposits,
grocery shopping and the rent
I need it to wash my clothes because just to wash a load
went up $1.75
and some may say well that ain't bad
but it is when I still need money for gas
and I would catch the bus
until they said it's about to be five dollars for an all day pass
and it's even worse to catch a cab
so instead of dealing with the public BS
I'll just deal with my own expensive convenience
I swear it's no way around it
the harder I work the broker my pockets
I'm telling you it's hard to upgrade
new necessities is like new accessories
when I get paid
never thought the root of all evil would make me say
it's time to get money
I need to get money
I've been trying to get this paper
ever since I got laid off
my bills still gotta get paid off
hustling trying to scrape up this paper
it's time to get money
I need to get money

for fancy restaurants, pimping up the ride for
club extravaganzas or just get away vacations
please
I need overtime on my two week vacation
just to catch up on my car payments
money I can't save it
especially when everyone's hand is out for the taking
that's why the poor stay broke
because people you don't even know you owe
and there's no other choice than to pay
because you can't afford a lawyer to fight the case
so instead we deal with what's important
like the fact that we need health insurance
but they ask for the endurance of my wallet
or wanting better schools for my kids
but it depends on the class of my pockets
it's like without the cash they won't even give you a chance
but like I say never hold your head down
and make the best of what you can
that's why I'm in the house still practicing my new dance
cause I'm a rock off when I'm accepted for them food stamps
still saying
it's time to get money
I need to get money
I've been trying to get this paper
ever since I got laid off
my bills still gotta get paid off
hustling trying to scrape up this paper
it's time to get money
I need to get money
for manicures, pedicures, days of rest with finest wine on chills
lets get real
I still need a new fingernail clipper
got holes in my slippers
drinking kool-aid with all my meals
I said it's hard out here
school ain't set me up with a career
trying to play by the rules

even when life don't play fair
so you can try and be slick
but you'll just get caught up in the politics
I know you thought you lost a lot
but you can be set up to lose all of it
if you want real talk
it doesn't matter what color is in the white house
or the official offices
they're color blind unless its elite money green
why do you think middle class issues are never seen
it's all a set up
pushing us down to the point we can't get up
well as of right now I'm fed up
I know we're more capable of being
dough boys just to get our bread up
we need to start taking what they won't give us
open our own business
invest in ourselves and stop taking on all of their expenses
see some things in this here life is a game
and you need to know how to play
and the number one rule is
if you ain't got dollars then you can't get change
and that's more than word play
it's everything they mean but something they'll never say

The Ugly Truth

My mind state is subliminal
These thoughts are unconditional
My conscious has no caution
And the outcome maybe critical (2×)
Triggered by society leaders
And So called important people
Who are blasphemers and cynical
More raw than Sunday school uncut
Practicing praise while juggling genitals
I said my mind state is subliminal
These thoughts are unconditional
My conscious has no caution
And the outcome maybe critical
Therefore I welcome you into the world of an ugly truth
Where a saint walks with sin in view
Because he became too impatient
To wait for God to handle Satan
That the prophet broke the prophecy and got physical
Started beating the uncommon sense out of society
And not giving a fuck if we were ridiculed
I mean what else are we suppose to do
When life's a bitch
And she's on her menstrual
She's on a cycle that never ends
The bleeding just gets heavier
And the cramps get more intense
And she's tired of the pain and the pressure
Of teaching her lesson
So she constantly contemplates suicide
But she knows she's not ready for Armageddon
See we are suppose to be using this time to see the signs
and become wise
But instead of gaining knowledge
We decide to pay for education
How are we suppose to pay for progression in a recession
When it's not worth the value in which they claimed it

This has become national highway robbery with arrangements
See you can either call Sally Mae and make payments
Or the state and federal will garnish your wages
And I know this has been said many times before
But some things need to be reiterated
On societys BS I could write chapters
But I'd rather spit money bars and watch these niggas go bananas
And if I ever stop spitting it's because I ate too many crackers
And you can take it how you want it
But I'm a colorblind bastard
Who takes it all for face value
And I see most of these niggas as assassins
See when life is threatened we tend to take chances
See life has no ransom so war is the answer
And when purpose becomes the question
I draw a blank and smoke mics like I want cancer
See this is rage mixed with passion
Sane insanity throwing a tantrum
In order to LIVE I had to learn to spell that motherfucker backwards
(EVIL)
So I could understand what I was dealing with
See I couldn't go HAM (Hard as a motherfucker)
like a nigga that just got out of jail
I had to go HAS (Hard as shit)
as a supplement
See I'm a nut with a case and I never lost it
And since it cost to get past minimum wage
Makes a nigga want to set it off
And I usually don't gamble but this is for all or for nothing
So by the time I'm done best believe I want my budget
To be fuck it
I want my bank account to be flooded
I want my ends to be so well versed that when money talks
I ain't never gotta change the subject
See they don't call me the ugly truth for nothing
Because I deliver more brain than a side hoe
When your main chick bluffing
Ima penetrate your mind until your neck sore

Stimulate all senses and make you bust out your pores
And I'll have you making ugly faces
With mind fornication
I said my mind state is subliminal
These thoughts are unconditional
My conscious has no caution
And the outcome maybe critical
Which means my mind is a dangerous place to be
So enter carefully
Or you could seriously become a casualty
Because Ima say what I want like a Spencers graphic tee
This is the Ugly Truth
The other me…

- The poor are prospects
for projects
a gentrification process
that sells genocide products
that consistently breeds consumers
a business boomer
that enslaved freedom -

The Blacks in Wax

Learning was scarce for the blacks
that's why we have the blacks in wax
which gives the clues and the facts
of why our blacks couldn't roam in packs
here's a place that shows what our forefathers have gone through
and when we don't show respect it is pitiful

Black Like Me

Black like me is what you want to be
co-existing and not entirely free
walking proud and erect
not scared of the world
each day showing my kinky hair
not a blond pressed curl
my lips are full
my hips are wide
my color is intimidating
I put fear into their eyes
when I walk past
I make every brother rise
and I, I am not disguised
for I am clearly seen
I need no mask to hide
I stand proud I define the word pride
you can call me black stallion
because messing with me you were destined
for a wild ride
they call me sister
and the others are called brothers
and when you put us together
we become your nationwide color
I am the ink that you write with
and the color of durable leather that lasts for years
I am the finished product called a diamond
that brings your wife tears
I am that black coffee in the morning
that tastes so good and keeps you going
I am the color of the cover of your bibles
that withhold all of God's words
that are true and vital
I am what everyone wants to be
strong, proud, and
Black like me

Being Black

Someone asked me
how is it being black
and I told him to go back over a hundred years
and ask the scars on my great great grandmothers back
and then I asked
If he could keep track
of all of my brothers and sisters that were hung
or of all of the sorrow songs that were sung
or all of those freedom fighting days
and today it only equals up to one month
I asked him if he could tell me
about how it is
when you're separated from your kids
you give life to a life whom with you does not live
or just didn't live at all
because the love of a black woman was too strong
to watch her child live like this
her love was too strong to let him get whipped like this
to get dismissed like this
she couldn't let this life live this life
because she knew that life is not this
so I told him to tell me how it would be
if he wasn't free
and he was told to live his life in slavery
not a human being but another mans property
and either picked crops or got beat
and where the lack of your knowledge was your own defeat
I said explain this
I said tell me how we were mislead by our own kin
to aboard slave ships
you ask me how being black is
so I tell you to imagine this
imagine how my past history
is still apart of my present
cause see the white man always
separated daddy from home

I wonder why today
daddy is never apart of my setting
see then he was sent away in chains
to a different plantation
today he's sent away in cuffs to a different prison
I guess that's why when mama was all alone
mama was so strong because mama
never really expected to stay with him
see that's exactly how it was in the beginning
it's the same song different rhythm
see they treat us like a game
and every time we play with them
but see I want you to get the bigger picture
because being black is more than just the negatives
positives come with it
see I want you to tell me
how this dumb foundation of beasts
set themselves free
and went places where people thought
they would never be
I want you to see how we never gave up
how we improvised for what we didn't have
and came close enough
and how we maintained our hustle
to make it through the struggle
so no matter how many times they broke us down
they made us bring a bigger huddle
and he asked me how it is being black
well I say it's wonderful
because people who make it through trial and tribulation
will always be considered as powerful

Revolution Revised

Open your eyes
this is the Revolution revised
we went from I's Be
to I be in less than a century
from yes sir I's got your paper
to yes sir I got you paper
years later we're still slaves
but now the situation gets bigger
because blacks ain't the only niggas
they took everyone with low income
and told them until you get some
call me masta' too
even from them with the blond hair
and those eyes that are blue
yea you, you a nigga too
and don't look at me crazy
because that's just truth
see the bare reality
is that the twin towers encompassed every nationality
probably every religion
but they say its a war on whether we're Muslim or Christian
none broke they all got a pot to piss in
so what's the question
well mines is why are we stuck in oblivion
to still vote
when the truth has been spoke
that this democracy of a nation
is not lead by democrats
but a dictatorship of leaders
who are eager to gain control
swallow this nation whole
and commit a Holocaust
higher than Hitler ever patrolled
wake up
this is the Revolution Revised
votes ain't save slaves the fight did

but I guess we're too afraid to fight
are we stuck in the wars excitement
or our own battles to pay attention
and now people say evict Bush and re elect Clinton
that'll solve the problem
that will loosen the tension
but see money talks
and he'll probably walk with them
we think everything is alright
until we wind up missing
pay attention
they're smart but see He's even smarter
a government without God is manslaughter
pay attention
a government without God is manslaughter
now take a look at us
we're not one nation under God it's invisible
U.S. is not under God
so they have no Guard
pay attention, listen
believe me, its real
it goes deeper than my mouth can spill
I mean they got me on myspace
so they can violate my space
if it wasn't for the networking then myspace I'd hate
I mean who's to say that Tom
ain't today's uncle Tom
it's too easy isn't it
but it's the easy that will blow right past us
and keep us in yesterday
see my mind has been full of rage
because common sense wasn't apart of my GPA
this is life
something that's never graded
it only counts when you've made it
past another day
see here's the truth gone naked
underground poetry is the Revised Revolution

see we started with the word
so we'll end with the word in conclusion
that's why the artist gotta stay on target with these rhymes
you pull out the glock be ready to cock it
and that be one of the top rules in gangsta logic
so if you ain't ready to come out in this heat of a Revolution
then stay your behind in the closet
and bear witness to the fight
open your eyes this is the Revolution Revised
truth against lies
we will rise
but as a people, one nation, under God,
will be visible

Attention

Attention my people
Now I don't mean to brag
And I don't mean to boast
But today I am proud to say
That I am your ghetto host
Now people let me introduce this
Creation into your world
They like to call her hoodrat
But she's better known as the ghetto girl
Now as she walks up and down the stage
You can see miss ghetto is fully equipped
With her head full of weave
And her purse firmly attached to the hip
Now people, please, don't be amused
Her skirt is really shorter than the heel size
Of her shoes
And watch out people
For Miss Ghetto is untamed and very wild
And beware when she opens her mouth
Because Miss Ghetto is very loud
And yes of course she does tame her children

As you watch how she curses
And look she just smacked her child
Yes Miss Ghettos mouth is very foul
Now as she walks off stage with all that exploited figure
Here struts down my homie, Mr. Ghetto Boy,
Better known as My Nigga!
Now here is a man who's not far from a boy
Who will use his AK47 as fast as a baby will
Play with his toys
And yes my nigga is fully stacked
With a pocket full of condoms
And A pocket full of weed
And will always tell the ladies
I can give you what you need
Yes ladies, please behold
The freshest Nigga that is oh so bold
And watch out he's a hungry one
He'll eat you out of house and home
And yes my nigga does freeload
And watch ladies how my Nigga will flex
And you might as well drop your panties now ladies
Because if my Nigga is not high then
He wants to have sex
And don't think he's little
Because my Nigga will always brag
About the size of his testicles
So ladies and gentlemen
The next time you need someone to get high, have sex,
Or just to lie about what he did
Please call 1-800-YOUR-NIG
And just to set the record straight
Your Nigga will be no less than 30 min late
Now as my nigga walks off stage
I would like to inform you
That this is how my black people are being labeled
At this time and age
They say we are lost, loud, morally insane,
And that we don't have respect for each other

Or our name
But I would like to say that we are more than society mentions
We are Not all Ghetto, we are Not all Niggas
And all of us do not work the pharmacy position
So let's change this so called tradition
And I thank you ladies and gentlemen
For all of your Attention

Self Revolution

Aren't you angry?
Aren't you pained?
Aren't you disappointed, disheartened,
Saddened?
For the recent occurrence of black peoples death
Have all been in vain
I know that regardless of how far we've came
I know that you feel like when America looks at you
They still see a slave
And I know that emotion alone is enough
To become enraged
I understand that when feeling attacked
It is natural instinct to fight back, burn, and break things
But remember people
that this is a system full of mind games
And we have been spoon fed into our current mind frame
For we have been patiently waiting for due process
That is long over due
Crazy when that's a process that a lot of our lost ones will never see
And Miranda yea they never heard of her
Because a cop has already become their murderer
However these are planned and plotted crime scenes
Is it just coincidence that Django,
The Butler, 12 years of Slaves, and Selma
All came out around the time that Travon Martin, Michael Brown, Eric
Gardner, and John Crawford got killed off
It seems to me like they use these movies to spark up ill feelings

Is it just coincidence that in the past few years
Everyone has become so got dag on afrocentric
That I seriously have to ask
When did the black panther party come back
And is it just me or on Social media
Do you also feel attacked
With racial stats
Trying to make you feel bad
for not focusing on being black
Like most of us ain't mixed
Like I am suppose to only focus on part of me
And not wholly express who I am
Is it just coincidence that this heated rash
Is being seen on mostly the middle and lower class
Funny how to this hate we are the only ones exposed
But see we are so accustomed to propagandas Willy lynching
That we don't even know when we're being strangled
Can't focus on ourselves when we are too busy
Focusing on the hate of someone else
Yet we are the ones killing each other
More than any other color or creed
See we have spoiled our own soil
And stopped growing trees that are evergreen
Instead we have become trees planted
Who like seasons they change
We have become the tree that springs
Up from the rain
But when summer comes all we do
Is show off our true colors and throw shade
And when the wind doesn't blow our way
We lose faith in our own branches
And our leaves of color fall for anything
So by the time winter arrives
It's no secret we grow cold
We become bitter, weak, we wither
So when push comes to shove we fall
See we are the tree that is easily pulled out of the ground
For we were never deeply rooted at all

But you can't build villages when they're full of broken homes
And you can't make black lives matter
When they don't care about life at all
And you can't put all your brown eggs
Into every colored basket you see
Because truth is
I know more brown rice trisket crackers
Than I know saltines
So go ahead and question me
Am I my brothers keeper?
Most definitely
But I will quickly become the Cain that Dis- Abled you
if you F with me
Because color won't make you my brother
Just like blood won't make you kin to me
See I must speak from the eyes of clarity
To help you understand that it should've saddened you
The way it saddened me
To watch bloods and crypts come together
To fight against a white man
So that they can continue to go on a nigga killing spree
See that's that shit that shouldn't make sense to you
The way it doesn't make sense to me
See this a mirrored revolution
Which means no real changed will come without self reflecting
To fix this type of hurt
You must be first sure of your self worth
Which means be pro self before anything
Be pro human being, pro all lives matter
See you need to take yourself out of that bowl of black cherries
And start complimenting that fruit salad
Crazy how even without the noose
We still wanna be strange fruit
Words that should've came from your pastor
But instead of teaching God's intentions
Like the fact that he said be fruitful and become many
Since the beginning
And the fact that the Bible never focused on color

But always focused on being human
He in turn for his own promotion fed black egos
To only intensify the hurt of a broken people
No wonder why there are so many non believers
When these preachers are nothing more than manipulating,
Hypocritical, motivational speakers
Nowadays you can find a Prophet in a poet
Before you find one in a so called religious leader
Understand that racism is just a figment of a bigger picture
Know that the governments intentions
Is to capitalize on new world order
Whose main objective is to keep us divided
So that we can remain dependent
If your community is broken
You can bet your top dollar that a politician won't fix it
I mean how would they survive if we didn't die
When they cash checks off our demise
So if I ever bear a child into this world
Whether it be precious boy or precious girl
I would inform them first and foremost
That hate is universal
Color will never be the only reason that the odds are against you
So never let racism be the reason that you are unsuccessful
Just focus on being an up standing human being
And positive karma will always bless you
Stay true to who you are
And never let the evils of this world consume your mind
Invest your time in aiming for the sky
And please remember my child
That no one I mean no one
Asks a star what color it is when it shines
It just shines
See Jesus didn't become king until after he was crucified
This proves that trials and tribulations come to those who
Are truly divine
They said the revolution would never be televised
And they were right
You will see it in the mirror

Taking place in your reflection
You may never change the world
But you will always be a strong link
To a positive chain reaction

~I am God's Creation
Nothing short of Great
Yet nowhere Near Greater
than the one who Created Me~

Decisions

A lot of times
it's hard for me to decide
because my mind can't make a choice
it's hard to hear my conscience sometimes
because of the distraction of another voice
another voice telling me all the time
what to do or what to wear
and how to wear my hair
all of these distractions make everything unclear
and sometimes it's my own mind that makes it hard
for me to decide
from the consequence and the fear of hurting my pride
all of these internal conflicts bunched inside
and from it I can't hide
I must make a choice
about my career
about my love
about my life
whether leading me to Dust or to Paradise

Stay on your Job

See if you lose your God
Then you lose your Guard
I know times are hard
Gotta stay on my Job
No matter the load
Don't lose control
Give it to God to hold
Gotta stay on my Job

Jesus Piece

See I know Gs that spend Gs on Jesus
To wear around their necks
Guns on their waistline
And wear bullet proof vest
Hold up gang signs
And put their brothers to death
These are the Gs that put our savior around their chest
Hypocritical servers of the Christ
Walk past his temple
Won't even pray at night
Sundays at their best
Mondays through Saturdays at their worst
At the temple there are no foul words
They wait till they walk up the street and around the corner to curse
See these Gs rock his piece
But don't support his peace
They just increase the deceased
He died with good will when he was beat
These Gs go to jail and get weak
They couldn't walk one foot in his feet
But they rock his piece
See these people confuse me
Because I thought Jesus was about resurrection
So I don't understand the bullet proof vest

If God is our protection
I need to ask you Gs to make a selection
Either you following these demons of hell
Or my God of heaven
Because you people got me stressing
Because you holler his name
But say detestable things in the following sentences
These phony, impersonating followers of the Christ
I bet you if they knew God would take their life
They would deny him twice
Lord these people that rock your piece ain't right
They drink your creation but don't do it in moderation
I guess they forget to adhere to your word in this occasion
And they always got excuses about why they do it
Say to get away from the pain
Is why they had to use it
I guess they ignore that God's word can alleviate the pain
Better than any herb they're abusing
They rock your chain
But your word they're refusing
All caught up in the devils confusion
And it's only on certain occasions when they try to repent
It always seems to be when they think they are about to face judgment
That's when they try to read your Bible
They try to take in your word like they want it
But the next day they do the same thing fronting
I don't understand how you can represent a man you don't follow
Wear the chain of a heart so full
And your's is so hollow
Suppose to be like Job
But you're more like Judas
Wearing a chain is like kissing up to the man
He expected as a disciple to lose you
Or Gs do I need to break it down like 50 cent
And ask you 21 questions about why you wear his chain
But don't follow him
That's like wearing a blue or red scarf
And you ain't neither blood or crypt

Or waiving the flag of a country you don't represent
So to a true Godfather you try to be gangster
But you're just a prankster trying to be a star
Bragging about bullet wounds and scars
But that ain't nothing to the bruises, broken bones,
Split flesh, scars, and death of my God
This G you wear around your neck died
For his people our sins and even the ones who did him in
And you so called Gs won't even take a shot for your men
And he takes care of all his children
And he has over a billion
And he's always there
To answer his children when they call him in prayer
But when one of your children call
Like a punk you run scared
You ain't never there
But like a G you rock his piece
And you ain't nowhere near the provider you need to be
These Gs spend Gs on Jesus like he's the new fashion
Saying they represent God
But they got their whole set clashing
Because the piece on the outside
Doesn't match the heart that's within
Spending all their hard working money
On big businesses of men
And a piece of their time they won't even spend on him
So until you become real Gs
Meaning Genuine
Don't rock his piece or tattoo your body with his picture
Just open your Bible and follow in his scripture
Because you don't have to spend Gs on Jesus
To be a G like him
Amen!

Devils Conversation

Let me tell you how I spoke to the devil
You know the leader of the rebels
The one that causes all the trouble
Well one day while I was reminiscing
And on my couch I was probably sitting
I know in positive thought I was chilling
Don't know the exact date or time
So I won't give it
But one day the devil had me tripping
he tried to open my door and let sin in
See the devil and sin are like brothers
You can't have one without the other
And the worst thing about the two
Is that they're always undercover
So when this random conversation arised
The devil was in disguise
So him I didn't recognize
Plus he came to me like a friend
So true and genuine
You wouldn't have known it was him
I mean the vibe was so close
It was like we were related
It was like he read my story and filled up my blank pages
I mean this conversation was outrageous
Because it was like he read my mind
See the devil knew that I was weak at this time
Because struggling and hardships had basically swallowed my pride
So he took me for a ride
And it was getting late in the day
And I was still OK but the devil started taking me down dark alleyways
So we drove to a spot that wasn't all that crowded
With bare trees and vacant houses
And we sat there chilling
Not saying a word
When out of the blue he introduced me to herb
He said now herb is what you call him

But his real name is marijuana
Now I'm a take a puff but you can hit it if you wanna
See I advise you to take a hit
Because it came from God's earth so you know that it's legit
And the government just don't want you to cop it
Because they only wanna make a profit
Like I said before God made the herb legit
So don't worry about the words of the government
Plus you not selling you just smoking it
And after one hit you can quit
Because I'm not a man to make you do it
But your problems Marijuana will help you get through it
Everything that's been getting on your nerves you will soon forget
Plus it takes you on a natural high
Takes from the ground to the sky
Mellowing out your mind
Through a cycle that makes you one with God
Now I know this may seem odd but Ms. Mary Jane does her job
She cures them all
Now there is a possibility that you can get addicted
But who wouldn't want to get addicted
To something that cures your sickness
Now I agreed I thought Marijuana was ill
But see i just wanted to chill
I didn't wanna take that thrill
So we chilled and kept still
And then he called back out to me
And said well because you don't want the weed
I'm a give you what you need I'm a introduce you to Hennessy
So you watch me and then you follow
I'll take a sip you take a swallow
And then we'll gulp the whole bottle
Now I know on a regular occasion we would drink this in moderation
But this is a different situation
See you need to drink this to drown out your sorrows
Believe me you'll be feeling better when you wake up by tomorrow
I mean first you'll get a little tipsy
Then you'll get a little sleepy

But this one drink can put you at peace D
I mean to drink this is not a crime
I mean Jesus turned water into wine
And I drink it all the time and I'm just fine
So here just take a try mellow out your mind
Now i felt a little skeptical
But what he said made sense to me y'all
I mean wouldn't it sound good to you
If he said Jesus didn't just drank it
But he made it too
So I did what a lot of people would do
I took a sip and a couple of other hits
But after that I quit
Now this was far from the end
The night had just began
And I had officially been introduced to sin
See he crept into me disguised as a fluid
And I can't give no excuses except I didn't mean to do it
But before I even knew what I did was wrong
Or even against the law
We spun off and hit another spot
Where there was a lot of people I mean the place was hot
I mean there was good food, good music,
I mean the place was so peaceful
But little did I know that lurking after me were his demons
See they were disguised in the costumes of fine men
Who acted like they wanted to get to know the person from within
When really within me is what they wanted to get in
But one did catch my eye
Now he was really fine
This dude was a dollar way far from a dime
So we had a little conversation and it was so innocent
I mean I really started feeling him
I mean he wasn't like any other man
I mean this dude was a gentleman
Or at least that's what I thought
Because after a few hours in his house i was caught
And while this so called gentleman was whispering in my ear

The devil started talking to me right in my head
Saying go ahead don't be scared
He doesn't want to take advantage
Just fill you up with passion to a place that is everlasting
So I had become just like Eve
By the devil I was deceived
Because I sank my teeth right into the forbidden fruit
In order to be pleased
And for that I was kicked right out of the garden of virginity
Because of God's words I didn't take heed
So I had become the victim
of the words of the devil
I had become a sinner
On a minor level
But a sin is a sin and on my knees I must repent
And ask God to forgive me for all of my sins
And as I ask for that I will ask for this
The gift to be wise
So the next time I can see through the Devils' disguise
Now whether this story is the truth or a lie
This is really how sin gets to you every time
See it's been shown from Genesis to Revelation
How The Devil feeds weak mouths with his temptation
Getting us all to commit sin with deception of his conversation

Where do I Go From Here

Where do I go from here
while I'm in high school sitting on my last year
searching for a college
to enhance my career
where do I go from here
while my father is incarcerated
the jailbird locked in a cage
the one I can't say I love or hated
because to me it was only semen he donated
I guess for that he should be appreciated
where do I go from here
when mommy is all alone
raising four kids on her own
trying to turn this broken down house into a home
where do I go from here
when I was stressed and depressed
from family and friends
I thought the bond would never end
but as heartaches began
my friends became friendless
something ended that I thought was endless
where do I go from here
when love is gone
and it's not coming back
two hearts separated on a one way track
and there's nothing to make up
for what your heart lacks
so in a mindless maze you're trapped
wondering…
where do I go from here
my brother in jail without bail
they said it was a throat that he had slit
yeah it was a crime
but did he really commit it
they said it was a black guy, white t, under a fitted
but is that enough description

to say that he did it
so in jail he's stuck sitting
saying
where do I go from here
this is for my people in war
who don't know what they're there for
they just know that overseas they were sent
told to fight for this country
when it's really for the government
but who knows the governments intent
because it's definitely not for the countries benefit
so while the soldier holds a gun up to the face of the innocent
he's stuck thinking
where do I go from here
for all my people that are broken down and beaten
and a true lord is what they are seeking
but at the last church they were at
the Pastor was doing dirt with the Deccan
saying he's a disciple of God
while he's making packs with the demons
mind you it's in the same place where he's doing his preaching
and you're wondering if you can believe in
the words that he's speaking
so once again for a true lord you're stuck seeking
looking up to the heavens and screaming
where do I go from here
this question is what people are asking
when they're down and out
when the gas and electric is out
when the rent is way past due
and everyone in the house needs a new pair of shoes
and they're literally sitting there wishing for Christmas
because that's the only time they can get
what they need to be getting
when there's an emergency and we dial 911
and the result becomes that not cops come
but when we decide to take vengeance
that's when they come to put us in prison

my people are asking
when the telephone is disconnected
and this is the 5th job application that has been rejected
when the bank teller has denied you a loan
and the home seller says no to your home
when the childrens parents are long gone
and they're all alone
when everyday we're scared to watch the news
and everyday they talk about the war that's surrounding Iraq
but what about the war that's surrounding you
where do you go
and what do you do
when we play this game called life and lose
see but God gave me the ability to choose
put Satan in this world and told him do you
and he didn't do that to be mean
he did that to test us
to see what we would do with Satan
as our pressure
and he didn't leave us here alone
see this great God left us his message
he gave us the Bible to guide us and help us
told us he would fight the war of Armageddon
told us if we stay true to him
when we die he would resurrect us
told us if we look deep within his word
we would find all the answers to our questions
see but societys people are only for self
they avoid the hand that is raised for help
so to me it was made very clear
why when I asked where do I go from here
and society replied I don't care
or even when I changed the question around
and asked from here where do I go
they gave me a different answer same concept though
they hollered I don't know
that's why I only have faith in my father the most high
because I didn't even have to ask him twice

in his answer
he gave me visions and filled my eyes with sights
he told in every situation you go through be a follower of Christ
and the place you will go from here my child is paradise

~ You can be Pharaoh King
But I'd rather be Moses
Leading my people across red seas
Because a Prophet always Profits past the Pockets
A Prophet always Profits past the Pockets
A Prophet always Profits past the Pockets
A Prophet always Profits past the Pockets ~

Metamorphosis

This is the metamorphosis
And of course it's just at it's beginning
But it's time to stop pretending
And start admitting that we have been sinning
See it's time to transform our ways
Please hint that I did not say change
For the concept of that is strange
For change is only making movements
To go back from whence we came
That's why we have to make a transformation
Which takes time therefore more patience
And perseverance on this occasion
Especially when you're dealing with Satan
Because he's just waiting
For the time, date, and place when
We slip up
Just saying Ima change ain't enough
Because the devil is calling your bluff
24/7, 365 days of the year when you're sleeping
So you better wake up
Because it's time to evolve

From a mustard seed that grew into a tree
That bloomed flowers y'all
From a squealing mouse into a lions roar
From a rugged rock into a shining diamond
That you see in the jewelry stores
From a caterpillar to a butterfly
We must also Metamorphosize
Because judgment day is coming
And time is running
Yes time is running out of this race
But we can catch up
All we need is the want, drive, and most of all faith
And with that God will help to make
the Metamorphosis take place
Because it's time to become who we are to be
A follower of the J.E.S.U.S C.H.R.I.S.T
So who's with me
Who's gonna help me take these measures to the extreme
Help me turn this drugged out junkie
Into a God fearing fiend
The crippled into a miracle motive machine
The blind to see
The chained to be set free
Give a clear conscious to those who use to live in fear like me
Lets go from a broken heart
To a heart beyond mended
From a mere imperfect sinner
To a person where perfection is always attempted
From dead to resurrected
Let a new life be embedded in me
Mere change will not set me free
Because I can change
And still want what I use to be
But the metamorphosis is key
To help unlock the new in me
So help me,
Help me to help those to move on
And never look back, Never look back

God said move on and Don't Look Back!
Because if you do then you will become a pillar of salt too
So lets move on
And become who we are to be
Change is not enough
For Him I will go through the extreme
Hands up, head bowed, on my knees
Repenting asking for forgiveness please
I'm tired of pretending
Truth is Father I have been Sinning
See I know this is just the beginning
But I realize where the end is
My time has come father
I'm ready for the Metamorphosis

~I pray that in my times of Sin
you rescue the Saint in me~

Forgive me Father

They wanna teach me about God
And I say I have already Jehovah Witnessed him
And he told me to stay Awake in the Watchtower
He said let the Holy Scriptures
Be your everyday agenda
And don't be afraid to share the good news
Please share the good news
That if you accept me Jehovah as your God
Due to my Son's sacrifice
You will never need to worry about an afterlife
For you will forever to time indefinite inherit paradise
And I wanna be there
I wanna live the way God intended
But everyday I find myself nibbling away
At fruits that are forbidden
Sometimes I knew that the fruits weren't for me

Sometimes I didn't
Therefore I humbly ask you to forgive me Father
For times that I know exactly what I do
Rebelling against your word
Even though my intentions are good
While lurking through darkness
Please know that my heart was always searching for you
So please forgive me Father
For I am sin
born and bred this way
Lead astray consistently
With the wish that I wasn't
With the hope that the impurities of my flesh
Wouldn't change the fact that my heart
Always belonged to you
That from day one I Always thought of you
That even up to now at this very moment
I still beg for your mercy
For I am sin
Born and bred this way
For my temple is a host of imperfections
Trying to be perfect for you
Wishing for your return
Praying that you won't leave me to burn with the ruins
Your heart I have always been pursuing
The best way I know how
In a world full of adversity, questions, and doubts
I have still been fighting for you
To know, to understand, to praise
While still trying to figure out myself
So forgive me Father
For I am sin
Born and bred this way
Cursed as soon as I was created
Descendants of the first sinners
To paradise there is no smooth pavement
So please forgive me Father
For who I am

A frustrated child in tears
Feeling like this struggle isn't fair
For I never asked to be here
I never asked to be born this way
To be broke and hungry
I didn't ask to be gay
I didn't asked to be molested and raped
I didn't ask to be the color of hate
I didn't ask for my parents afflictions
I didn't ask for the alcohol and drug addictions
I didn't ask for the deficiencies and deformities
I didn't ask to be the chooser between a million
Different religions
Of sin Father
I didn't ask to be the victim
In the trenches of this world Father
I just ask to be forgiven
For I am sin
A curse that I was given
And A curse that I hate to accept
In my daily repentance

Judgment

Don't worry about those who judge you
Especially when they don't know you
And it really doesn't matter what they say
Because we're all gonna be judged on judgment day

~Born into the Devil's world
expected to follow God's laws
I wasn't only born a bastard
I was born an oxymoron~

~Once you've underestimated the possibility
then you have ignored God's Capability~

~As the world turns and the seasons shift
as we lose and regain consciousness
as every action causes a reaction
repercussion or a consequence
remember time is in progression and of the essence
as we come closer to the days of Armageddon ~

Motivation

Motivation

"Take your dreams off of layaway. They were not meant to be bought, nor sold or put on hold. They were meant to live." My mother once told me this. As we all know life is too short to take for granted. Too short to let someone else box and label your package. Too short to let your pottery be molded by another mans' hands when God gave you free will! Within you is the power to think and create for yourself. You alone possess the power to make great things happen. If any of this sounds absurd understand that Crazy is a Genius. Most people don't understand the gifts that they weren't granted. However don't let their lack of comprehension keep you from opening yours. In fact I implore that you not only open but utilize your gift. I implore you to take chances and to believe in yourself. I implore you to remove yourself from negative situations. I implore you to cry so that you may smile and laugh. At times I implore you to let your mind live vicariously through your heart. I implore you to be open minded enough to know that there is so much more than you. Yet focused enough to realize that you are it. You matter, and so does your song. So much so that we want to hear you sing, so that we can enjoy and remember every moment that we sung along. Instead of listening to someone else's version of your music that could never live up to who you are.

My Song

My song of plenty years
not longer than many
but pretty longer than some
surprised I'm still living
because I almost died young
it's a blessing to hear me singing
instead of someone else listening
to my song being sung

My Name

My name My name
it will always stay the same
and it's not going to change
or be turned into a game
my name is different from all the rest
and to me my name is the very best
I know you might disagree
but my name is very special to me
I do declare but not in despair
that everyone should hear from ear to ear
that this is my name
and it's not going to change
because I love my name
oh yes I do
and I hope you feel the same about your
name too

Happy

Happy is when you're filled with joy
it's like giving a child a brand new toy
happy is when your fright is no longer fear
happy is when you're filled with cheer
happy is when you're ready to rejoice
with either a high or low voice
happy is when your face is filled with a smile
sometimes it only lasts for a little while
happiness gives you a warm spot inside
happiness makes you filled with pride
happiness is going to stay here forever
and people should be happy together

Nothing but your Personality

Your color doesn't faze me
neither does your shape faze me
but your personality fazes me
your color and your shape could be there
but your personality tells me if you're really sincere
your money doesn't faze me
neither does your clothes
but I would like to see a personality as beautiful as those

Never say Never

Never say never
because you never knew you would do
the things you wouldn't expect to
and the things you expect to do
you never do
so never say never
because only time will show
unless you say I never know

Giving up

Giving up on you
giving up on me
giving up on us
giving up on we
giving up on family
giving up on friends
giving up on the beginning
giving up on the end
giving up on love
giving up on joy
giving up on the girl
giving up on the boy
giving up on the best
giving up the worst
giving up on the pain
giving up the hurt
giving up means I have nothing left except
when I give up on life
I receive and give into death

You Can Hate

They say haters will never prosper
they will only make life worse
there have been haters hating
before the world itself
hating on me because I'm known
and they're the unread book on a barren shelf
they hate on the way I walk,
the way I talk,
the way God made me
haters talk about everything they claim they saw
but I'm afraid they can't see
you can tell a hater from a mile away
because they stick to you like glue
always got something negative to say
no matter what wrong or right you may do

Young Poem Writer

Young poem writer as yellow as gold
I heard that you write with your whole heart and soul
I heard you write about today
and what the future will bring
and how winter changes to spring
young poem writer so delicate and sweet
I heard you write about people on the street
I heard you write about human kind
and different things that comes upon humans minds
young poem writer I heard that your poems
were different from everyone else
and I heard you would be very famous
young poem writer keep on writing this way
and I will look up to you everyday

My Dream

Dreams unheard, unseen, not read
The only dream is the one in my head
My Dream to succeed and strive
My Dream to live faithfully in God's eyes
My Dream of a friend never lost
My Dream to live with no cost
My Dream to speak throughout the nation
With only two utensils a pen and a paper
My Dream just to make it through the day
Without paying the prices
I have to pay

Young Child

Young Child so meek and mild
Why is there always a frown
 and never a smile
Why would you rather study than play
And why is this done everyday
Would you consider to have some fun
When all your work is neatly done
Would you like to get up and say
May I play May I play
Wouldn't you like to live an experienced life
Before your death strikes
Young Child be a child
And have a reason to live your life
So have some fun
Like one who is young

Tear me Down

I stand tall and with your whip
You try to tear me down
And when I fall
I wipe the dirt off my knees
From off the ground
My body is weak but my spirit is strong
To withstand this burden of mine
When will slavery be over I ask
But there is no set date and time
My tongue speaks the words
That you don't understand
So you call me nigger
Instead of who I really am
I start to find light
And I know the light inside of me will grow
And when you start to see that light
You take all my hopes and dreams
Play around with them
And then like a balloon you let them go
I do have dreams
and I know that my dreams will come true
And when it happens there's nothing you can do
Physically you tear down my strength, my body,
But not my heart
Because spiritually there is nothing you
Can tear up, down, or apart

Now or Never

I got to live for each day
Because I might not wake up tomorrow
Bring the best out of joy
And remember all sorrows
Can't live in one spot
I have to be on my way
I mean just because I woke up this morning
Doesn't mean I'm going to wake up
The next day
I can't stop time
Therefore time is my issue
I can't sit up here and wait
So if you're not coming
Well I'll miss you
I can't talk about doing
Therefore I must do it
Because if I sit up here talking
Then I'm making my time useless
So I must make each day
A day worth living
And make sure each hand I'm dealt
I play in good decision
Because the game won't go on forever
So I either play
Now
Or
Never

Ambition

There is a force by which we all are driven
and the word for this force is ambition
this force is the power that causes us to strive
to make it through the day
and to stay alive
such power does this ambition withhold
and the happiness is the
success you feel
once you've reached your goal
though with each force there comes
friction
the opposite force that tries to lower
my ambition
but the drive I have is way too strong
it's the force that helps me to carry on
though no matter the conflict
no matter the friction
there is a force by which we are driven
and the word for this force
can only be called ambition

Hip-Hop

Hip-Hop is
50 cent with nine shots by the glock
listening to Biggie and vibing to Tupac
and his lyrical poetry
yet knowingly hip-hop is
Snoop Dogg and Dr. Dre
NWA
Funk Flex, Run DMC and Jam Master Jay
that was back in the day
where we started with beat box and pop lock
and used five-o to describe cops
Hip-Hop is big gold chains
platinum and bling bling
speaking in a language we call slang
Hip- Hop is so much more
yet all these things
Hip-Hop is representing our hood
from North, South, East, West
and showing off different meanings
with tattoos across the chest
Hip- Hop is engaging in lyrical battles
to show who's the best
but it's not all about the contest
it's about spitting out true issues with one mic
bringing diversity to unite
showing our differences and emotions
with words instead of the fight
Hip-Hop is
how black people get hype

The Game

This is my reason for living
it's either my crossover or the hard passes I'm giving
and each play
makes my day
once I touch the rock
I catch adrenaline and it won't stop
and oh boy don't let me get hot
because if you give me the ball every shot I'll pop
then there's the crowd
I love them when they get loud
whether it's the whoos or the boos
it's the spirit that gets you to do what you do
and each time I'm on the court all pressures leave
it's something about the game that makes me feel relieved
but what I love most about the game are the tricks
the hardest part is when I get your neck
dag I got you and your man
thought I shot but the ball never left my hand
and there goes my man back door
give him the ally and he dunks it beautifully
and you might as well leave because your team is done for
and whether it's in the gym or the streets
I love it when a one on one meets
it's just me and you
and it's funny with the things I do
I take a little A.I. think I'm about to go
but I bring you right back
and don't try to play it off
I heard them ankles crack
and after that's done I mix it with some and one
I know you're burnt
so let me take you out the oven cause you're done
man every dribble and swish sounds like it calls my name
you can't tell me I don't love this game

Minors

This boy wouldn't show love in public
but these girls they loved it
behind closed doors he treated sex as a subject
all these girls he would study for class
as he told them to put down their heads
and put up there... yeah
then he would pull down his pants
and put on a condom
thinking he wouldn't catch crabs
this little boy he was moving too fast
a 13 year old boy trying to become a man
and it's not just the little boys
it's the little girls
who still wear ponytails and curls
who be practicing different positions
and you know I'm just wondering if
these parents are listening
because it's getting ridiculous
how these kids get influenced
by you, the tv and internet
I mean this situation got me tripping
these kids lose their virginity
in the matter of seconds
and it's these adolescents
we need to question
girls say they do it because of depression
and boys do it because of the pressure
or maybe they are looking for love
in the wrong direction
this is just what I'm guessing
I guess that catching a disease is
how they will learn their lesson
but the promotion of it is truly the confession
but they don't promote disease
about Aids, HIV, and STDs
they think they're receiving pleasure

when they're only getting pleased
with soon to be tragedies that a child doesn't need
or are they being blessed with a seed
and they don't even understand their blessing
because the situation is so stressing
and it's sad when they don't even know
until they begin to show
their belly grows
their friends now know
and behind closed doors they are
being called hoes
watch mistake after mistake unfold
and she can't take care of the baby alone
so to get an abortion is what she is told
it seems like for every pleasurable fantasy
that is being fulfilled
there is another child to be killed
when will this generation be healed
I guess they were waiting for the truth to be spilled
kids getting so caught up with this free will
or the thrill
of sex weed and the pill
these minors think that it's a game
they don't know that it's for real
they don't understand that the future
is what they will reveal
and the generation from before
don't make it no better
when will you teach your kids
that sex doesn't always equal pleasure
and the weed and the pill will make you ill
and the liquor can cure your sickness
but too much of it can kill
we need to put these children in check
show them the basics of cause and effect
because it's not the mentality
but the drive that they lack
it's a shame how great minds are wasted

because they weren't taught the basics
they got a whole bowl of sense
they just won't put their pinky in and taste it
and it's because these parents won't make them
parents stop leading your kids down the road
for the devil to take them
instead give these kids the ability to learn
so that their first word is not a curse word
and teach them how to add and subtract
more than crack from bags
and how to open their minds
before their legs
and how to unite, together as people
and not their nose to the pipe
people don't take these minors light
because they are the ones that determine your life
they are soon to be doctors, lawyers, bank tellers,
they are to be scholars
parents teach your children
because our future lies in the arms of the minors

Suicide

Why?
I'm sorry...
I love you...
Amen...
They are a synchronized orchestra
Walking past you everyday
Playing their hymns of plea
For a reason, for one reason
For a reason we heard of many times before
Through tragedies, struggles, and slammed doors
Hard but we moved on or kept trying
Sometimes we even proved triumphant
While others get stagnant
Paralyzed in miserable moments

Where the devil owns them
And there is no room for dreams
No chance of prevailing is how it seems
Through push and prayer
There's no miracle for you
And we look at them with confused
Yet concerned faces
Saying baby you can make It
There is always a reason to...
FLASH!!
Transferred e.g. #1 a kid
A young girl who walks dead
Who lives with a drugged mother
And no father at age 6
Sold to a man for the worth of a fix
At school she is silent
Called upon for questioning
But remains quiet
Look you have to pay attention
You can hear the frustration of the teacher
But never once looking into her eyes
Realizing the situation goes deeper
For the kin of sleep seeks her
And only she can feel him
She says quietly sleep voice trembling
But because she has a whole class
And one student can't have all her concentration
She says awe baby you can make It
See we feel there is always a reason to...
FLASH!!!
Transferred e.g. #2
Bruised
Because others say their sexual
Preference is confused
Maybe true
So they are battered outlandishly
Never realizing their preference
Maybe due to past crisis issues

For instance she was raped
So she finds comfort behind the baggy clothes
She is safe
And he truly believes that she is
Who he should be
Or some are in between what we see
And medical issues
The complications are far more than mental
So because we are ignorant to what they've been through
We say baby you can make it...
There is always a reason to...
FLASH!!!
Transferred e.g. #3
The reflection in the mirror and who do I see
The image that looks back
Is the image of me
Repressed memories come back for the haunting
Grade school, middle school,
I can hear the kids taunting
But even beyond the kids
I fast forward to that place
That we try to erase where all neglect you
After you fought so hard to prove your part
All dismiss you
Questioning your purpose
Hurt feelings resurface
As you think of lifes mission
Contemplating my decisions
Of whether I should keep running this race
Or if I should end it
Looking at me
As if the thought ain't never hit them
They say
Awe baby you can make It
There is always a reason to...
FLASH!!!
Transferred e.g. #4
My last door I explore

They symphony playing in harmony
For they play the hymns of losing another
She lost her brother, he lost his mother
And the only way back to them is death
And she can't be without him
And he without her
Vows didn't have to be said
In order for the commitment to be
until death do us part
Being a hardworking human
Doing the best that you can
But through permanent and temporary laid off
Bills that can't get paid off
Food isn't easy to scrape up
So life without paper
Makes some feel less than what they are made of
So at times I know you don't want to wake up
BUT WAKE UP
Because the money, bills, jobs, and others
Don't make us
So never let the evils of this
World break us
Because I hear you all synchronized
The orchestra I hear your hymns of plea
Just to be alive
Even though you contemplate suicide
Let God be your guide
There is a book on this earth
That He provides to all his kids
Open it and I promise
You will always find your reason to live!

Poetic Therapy

Pain & Struggle
Anger & Anguish
Hurt & Strain
Now this is therapy
I Promise
We cry when we're born
and we laugh in the face of death
scared by the light of life
peace after dark I rest
now if you can look into the eyes of a lone soldier
and make a mental note out of his mess
it will add therapy to the life you lead
I promise, I promise
I promise like... like
he said till death do us part
and they put on their rings
like friends forever who give dap
and mark the tree with their blood stains
like the promise of God
when he said the death of mankind do to deluge
will be no more
I am the rainbow, the sign of that promise
after the rain pours
I am signature
bonded contract
official like prophets
for the prophecy that I spit
will only take place if you take time
to nurture it
life I remember when I was in search of it
didn't know the worth of it
what the purpose is
innocent ignorance
lead me to believe I was the curse of it
happiness thought I could purchase it
until I understood the worth of pricelessness

and I became the words on a page written by two
set a blaze to vanish never again to view
I became the worth of that secret
and I intend to keep it
I mean it
please understand the things you are about to see
I may have already seen it
may send your soul to freedom
when you feel like your alone
and you might need them
words of empathy alone give comfort
to a soul feeling defeated
lost battles give you strength for the war
it's time to beat them
get to know your enemy
shake his hand politely greet him
for this well known fact
that if you keep him in your for front
you'll see when he tries to stab you in the back
remember the world is on the prowl
and you are the prey
due to hate with lack of reason
life is a consistent struggle jungle
and it's always hunting season
they say don't cheat the game
or renege on the hand you're dealt
but how can you play fair
when life ain't fair itself
now not to say I condone
intentional misplay of a bad hand
but to cheat at the game of life I understand
but I would rather deal with the hand I'm dealt
because karma's a bad man
and I know you're tired of suffering
from the headaches of the world they make you nauseous
but take a teaspoon of this poetic therapy
and you'll feel better
I promise

She Holds Her Own

She Holds Her Own
Every inch every pound
Doesn't need nobody
She has more than enough body to hold her down
So humble yet proud
That she holds her own
150 + pounds yet struts in her stilettos
Now that's talent
Give her the tight rope
because she has something to balance
And it's more than her figure
Along with the hips, bust, thighs, and butt
The insecurity from all of the criticism comes with it
But she refuses to lock herself
In starvations prison
She enjoys all the delicacies
She will never have an empty kitchen
See she doesn't fault herself for her metabolism
And embraces all of her thickness
See she knows she has that body with no restrictions
Opening her package is more like Christmas
And I appreciate what the gift is
She's the type to make you say
If this is not perfection
Then I'm attracted to your blemish
See malnourished niggas are the only
Ones scared to look at her frame
In fear of a bigger picture
See they have no idea what they're missing
But it's cool
Let them remain clueless
They don't need to understand
That the bigger the fruit the more juice it produces
See only a voluptuous mother hen
Could keep these chickens thirsty
And these jive turkeys drooling

Man I wonder how she does it
With everyone in her ear
Whether they're hating or they're lusting
Her body they want it
And since they can't have it
They taunt it
But she doesn't get mad
She just flaunts it
Does her tuck, lift, and rub it before she struts it
All before her public
Oh how I love it
They way she treats those boulders
Like chips on her shoulders
Watch how she eats them with class
Because what her body takes on
Many wouldn't be able to endure half
No wonder why they mad
Because she holds her own
See someone real wants something they can feel
See only dogs jump bones
And when you think about what her body embodies
Such a beautiful spirit
And a wonderful soul
The blessing of a woman is what your eyes will behold
So just know that for every one love
There are a million and one haters
And if they can't hold you down, every inch, every pound
Tell them skeletons to get their weight up

Omnipresent Goddess

Let me tell you about this
Bitch, Trick, Hoe, Slut
Winch, Whore, Pussy, Cunt, Thot
with a mind frame so thoughtless
that you get in the most Thotfull positions
facials are the only way you will ever watch his children
you disgust him
you bad bitch with gold digger ways
getting lost in Louis
revealing all your secrets that Victoria never kept
as Remy keeps you a rapunzeled princess
you hide behind Sephora and Mac
and then you Cover Girl yes you Cover Girl
all of who you are behind those colors girl
just to make up for who you aren't
and pretend who you ought to be
you cowardly lioness
you are societys slave
for only a bruised soul wants to be beat for days
but I guess that's just the method man
to a scar face
you are reason of sin
from the beginning you mingled with serpents
therefore you will be treated like Eve in evil
like the betrayer of Sampson
like the one who asked for his head upon a platter
you vindictive savage, you Jezebel
you deserve all the hurt and pain
as far as they can tell
you are useless ma'am
the only reason for you being
is for a mans relief and for you to bear another man
Vicious???
yeah, sad thing is, is that a lot of women
actually believe this
they own up to who people say they are

and allow themselves to be mistreated
mentally, physically, and emotionally beaten
loving him so much more than herself
that she succumbs to his secretion
all in hopes just to keep, a him,
around
everything she alters
without the hope of an altar
while still being called a bitch
for being the same dog that you are
she just bit harder
how dare you slain her name
when she is an Omnipresent Goddess
yes Omnipresent meaning being present
everywhere at the same time
usually referred to when speaking of God
but she is the finesse to what God is
she is an Omnipresent Goddess
yes she is literally everywhere at the same time
if you were to look within the windows of her soul
it is lit with moonlight
and her aura pierces of sunshine
you will be surrounded by her love
on a 24hr rotation
captivating is the way she mothers nature
for the lineage of humanity
lingers within her wombs
and the forgiveness of all sins
was birthed by her
Woman
yet you underestimate the power in who she is
she has been the blood of diamonds
you can see her shining every time
you look into the eyes of a kid
she is backbone even when a rib doesn't exist
she is the depth and mystery
that resides within the ocean
and the beauty that lies upon the surface

she is more than gift
she is the blessing that was asked for
which means she is more than worth it
she is deserving
to be more than what media makes her
although she isn't perfect
made out of God's image she is blessed
to be the finesse to what God is
for she is literally everywhere at the same time
an Omnipresent Goddess

Lone Wolf

I went outside
just to gaze at the moon
like a lone wolf
who strayed away from the pack
contemplating whether I
should keep walking away
or if I should be heading back
but after starring at the moon
until it disappeared
I decided to continue alone
for I am not the wolf who
walks among the pack
I am the wolf
who creates his own

Dream Chaser

They ask me
How do you Keep following your dreams?
I tell them...
To keep running,
Running like a barrel's on your back
Keep running,
Running like a barrel's on your back
Keep running forward,
I'm talking tunnel vision never looking back
Don't let that steel nightcap your realities
You only see dreams in your sleep
So stay woke
Keep moving and make the vision come true
Stop worrying about if someone hasn't done it yet
And accept the fact that the vision is for you
Even if it has been done trust that no one can do it quite
Like you do
See everyone got it twisted
Thinking they're chasing the dream
When really the dream is on a mission haunting you
Whether day or night it's taunting you
Just take a minute
And think about why your visions are more like premonitions
Why every decision you make towards it is more like intuition
Why every accident feels like intention
Why every roadblock is really a light bulb
Telling you to do it different
Fruition, that be the reason that the image is so clear
That you become scared of the view
Why the outcome of every action feels like deja vu
Understand that your steps have already been ordered
You just need your feet to follow suit
And if you still don't believe me then let these haters be your proof
Explain why there are so many people doubting
And underestimating you
Realize that if you really were a waist of time

Then no one would really be clocking you
But their clocks are out
And they're watching you
Because you are something to see
For many eyes stare at a dark sky for a long time
Awaiting a shooting star
just so they can wish on the success of your dreams
So keep running,
Running like a barrel's on your back
Keep running,
Running like a barrel's on your back
Keep running forward
I'm talking tunnel vision
Never looking back
Don't let that steel nightcap your realities
Instead let pessimism
Be the ammo to your glock the optimist
And prime all of your negative energy out of it
Because see this glock it rarely opts to miss
It just keeps aiming and shooting until the targets hit
See you have to keep aiming and shooting until the targets hit
But too often we deter ourselves from being determined
That's why you have to look yourself in the mirror
And preach your self sermon
And say self, say self I ain't gonna quit
Between dreams and reality purpose is my catalyst
See I know that the weapons will form against me
But they will not prosper
With you by my side self I am confident
See today I accept all the weight on my shoulders
That's how I acquire strength
Today I embrace all the tests and the challenges
For there is no better way to solidify what my knowledge is
See there is no mistaking
When your minds eyes has sought greatness
Fate is the only game you will lose by not playing
So as long as your game
I mean really there is no losing this

There is no reason for blisters to be in your feet
When these shoes they fit
So lace them up
And keep following your vision
Because it is the blueprint
And keep running,
Running like a barrel's on your back
Keep running
Running like a barrel's on your back
Keep running forward,
I'm talking tunnel vision never looking back
Because if you do you will pillar of salt your dreams
So keep moving and make the vision come true
Remember you are not chasing the dream
The dream is haunting you
Forcing you to follow your vision
For dreams are really purposeful prophecies that you must pursue
So keep running and grab hold of your realities
Without doubting
That the dream was meant for you

*~Anger only heightens negative energy
to gain positive energy you must first instill a calmness within
yourself~*

*~Learn to love tribulation
in order to master Triumph ~*

*~I use sense to make dollars
so that my dollars will never make cents
only true hustlers will get this~*

*~ I never stress the molehills
I gotta save my energy for the mountains~*

~Unplanned but on Purpose the definition of a bastard~

*~If you're digging for Gold keep digging
but if you're digging for something Golden
dig Deeper~*

*~Take what the world has to give
and give to the world all you have to offer~*

*~All the strength you used to knock me down
doesn't come close to the strength that I used
to get back up. So whose stronger?~*

*~There is no page that can hold me
and no title that can summarize
who I am til the death of me
I am a story never ending
so stop trying to read me
and just join the chapter while I'm living~*

*~Remember that when your life
becomes so busy with the unnecessary
it's probably blocking something great from happening.
So clear your schedule~*

*~There will never be good people in your world
if you don't take the initiative to be one~*

*~Keep going where most people have given up
and see how far it Gets you~*

~Sometimes your light shines too bright that it blinds people when they are
close to you. It isn't until they are
away from you that they can truly see how beautifully your
light shines! Some people are meant to love and adore you from afar. It takes
someone special to embrace the magnitude of your beauty up close~

~Good people continue to be Good people
even when the odds seem to be against you
even when they paint out your Truths to be lies
even when they make your good deeds seem evil
and even when the good in you feels defeated
continue to be good people
for the reward will outweigh your troubles
and your victory can never be taken once you win~

~When you're a lion all they see is Strength they
never really hear the pain in your Roar~

~When your sunsets someone else Sunrises and the cycle continues…
The bittersweet of the End always
tastes like new Beginnings~

~Be important enough today
that they couldn't wait until
tomorrow
for tomorrow is never promised
and promises are often broken
but today will forever be a present and the present will always be a gift~

~Remember at your worst you are still alive
with the ability to make a change~

*~Regardless of your age
you will never be a day over beautiful~*

*~Keep pushing
because a lot of people won't push you
everyone supports success
only a few support the struggle~*

*~ I commend the man who continues
to give his rib
for your faith is sure
that in giving pieces of yourself
you will become stronger than the man
you were before
I adore, I applaud, I love you~*

*~ When you are too lit to light
nobody can match you~*

*~ The only time I look down
is to watch them come up
pull them
so I can push them above me
and admire how they rise~
letter to my nephews and all the children I adore*

Crowned

Once again to all those known and unknown. Thank you! Your time and energy spent with me is very much appreciated. I hope that this voyage has met or even exceeded your expectations. More than that I hope that this voyage has taken your mind and soul to a gratifying place. A place where you were able to take precious gems along with you. If worthy please share with all the ones you know. Since writing and poetry has been my safe haven I have left two blank pages just for you. In hopes that you have felt inspired enough to write. It doesn't matter what it is. It could be a rap, a poem, a speech, a new idea, your dreams, your goals, your master plan, or even the beginning to your own book. Feel free to write your thoughts about this book whether good, bad, indifferent, or all of the above. Write for the difference that it will make in your life. The voyage will only end if you let it. So don't let your mind stop traveling. Instead continue on your journey through the Good, the Bad, and the Ugly until you reach your Truth! Thank you!

For You

For You